T0095530

ARE
BRITISHPOLICE
Institutionally Racist?

MEMOIRS OF AN ACCUSED CONMAN

SHUJAAT HUSAIN

authorHOUSE®

AuthorHouse™
1663 Liberty Drive
Bloomington, IN 47403
www.authorhouse.com
Phone: 1-800-839-8640

Published by AuthorHouse   07/17/2012

ISBN: 978-1-4772-1783-2 (sc)
ISBN: 978-1-4772-1784-9 (hc)
ISBN: 978-1-4685-0369-2 (e)

Introduction

It has been over six years since the saga with the police that is the premise of this memoir finally ended. The incident and the subsequent litigation seemed to take a heavy toll on me as more and more voices from amongst the police forces and their legal teams were making themselves heard. A few months after the judgment that finally brought me justice after a long uphill battle, my mother passed away in America. It was probably the saddest day of my life. Her passing dampened the feelings of elation I experienced from the tribunal success.

To think back and put down all events as they actually happened and to give one's reflections is not easy. I wanted to write down my memoirs in efforts to raise awareness of the danger posed by the police forces in the country. I was moved also by the numerous complaints of harassment and discrimination that have appeared in the British media, particularly the victimisation of Muslims. It appears that racism in the police forces is a commonplace occurrence and is almost taken for granted, the politicians and leaders of the forces frequently condoning it and appearing to justify it by, among other rationalisations, referring to society as "a melting pot". I, for one, am unable to agree at all with this notion.

Something concrete needs to be done to try to stem this demon from possessing most of British policemen. It was with this intention in mind that I decided to pen my experiences and thoughts based on my interaction with four of the forty three British Police forces. In my youth I had been advised by elders to be careful of the "white" Englishman and not to take him at face value. I never took this advice seriously. Not until my close encounters with the British Policemen, however, did the full significance of these words begin to dawn on me.

All views expressed are my own based on my experiences in the tribunals and elsewhere. I have to express gratitude to my daughter for proofreading part of the manuscript.

S. Husain
London
May 2012

One

The Arrest

Early days in January in any part of Britain tend to be the coldest of the year, and Cardiff in Wales was no exception, especially so during the first week of 2001. I had been in Britain for only the second successive winter and felt overly taken in by the arctic temperatures in my friend's home (where I was residing) located in the middle of Cardiff. As I got up in the early morning, I realised that the heating was not working and that, to add to the misery, the hot water wasn't on either. My friend, Ali, who, like me, had arrived from Karachi – he nearly one and a half decades before me – and worked as a constable for the local police. He had been kind enough to give me the only dwelling I could find during the hapless first months in the city. The apartment was a steamy, noisy place located above a chip shop.

I boiled water in the large pan on the electric stove to prepare for my morning shower. Though this was barely enough to turn the icy water just about lukewarm, I felt lucky enough to survive the ordeal. After having a rudimentary breakfast that consisted of boiled eggs, toast, and a pot of tea, I covered myself in the blanket and was watching the eleven o'clock news in the sitting room when my mobile phone rang.

"Shujaat, how are you?" Ali was on the line.

"I'm fine. How are you?" I replied.

"Are you comfortable?"

"I'm getting along. What's up? Are you at work?"

"Yes." Ali sounded a bit cold and distant. "Did you apply for a job with the Avon and Somerset Constabulary over in Bristol a couple of months ago?"

"Yes, I did," I answered slowly, thinking.

"Look, Shujaat, a detective constable and a sergeant from the Avon and Somerset Police want to speak to you regarding the job application. Can you go over to the Rumney Police Station tomorrow at 11.00 a.m. to meet them?"

"Yes, I can. Is this part of the job interview, Ali?" I queried.

"I really don't know. I've been asked to give you this message. So you'll show up there, wont you?"

"Yes, I will. Is there anything else on your mind?"

"No. All the best. I'll speak to you later."

"Bye, see you later." I hung up.

I began to think. I remembered somewhat vaguely applying to a job with the police forces some two months ago. The position was a non-uniformed job, somewhat routine, quite different from the uniformed one I was used to in Karachi. The job I had applied for was that of intelligence officer. Now I remembered well.

The next morning, after a somewhat early start to my usual routine, I put on my winter coat and took off to Rumney Police Station in my Rover. Thinking this was probably a different form of interview for the job opening, I was somewhat keen to meet the policemen Ali had spoken of.

The drive to the police station was not long. I parked my car in the parking lot and entered the station. The young female constable at the reception queried me, and upon my explanation of Ali's message of yesterday, she asked me to wait in the waiting area. I did as asked.

Within a few minutes, I saw two grim-looking, tall white men in suits and overcoats emerge from within the reception area. They asked me for my name and address. The slightly thinner one in the front introduced himself as Detective Sergeant David Jones and his colleague as Detective Constable Kenneth Colbeck of the Serious Fraud Department of Avon and Somerset Constabulary in Portishead. Sgt Jones appeared a bit softer to speak to, but DC Colbeck appeared to be styled more in the shape of the renowned British bobby – red necked, thick set, large sized, and scowling at me through his blue eyes. From their manner and body language, it appeared as though they were on one of the biggest missions of their lives!

As soon as I replied to his query, Sgt Jones took one or two steps towards me and asked me to come inside the police station from the reception area. As I moved in, he closed the door behind me and took out copies of what I recognised to be my job applications for positions with the Kent, South Wales, and Avon and Somerset police forces. He flung these before my face and asked me if this was my handwriting and if these were applications submitted by me to the three police forces. I confirmed that they were, and he immediately stated, "I'm arresting you for deception or attempted deception in making false statements in your job applications and CV to three British Police forces."

I was shocked to hear that I was being arrested. I couldn't, at that time, understand what the allegations were and was simply too taken aback to even reply to his assertions. Though he did not handcuff me, Sgt Jones took me to a back room and stated that I would have to go through the "procedure" for being placed under arrest. Shortly thereafter, I understood what this so-called procedure meant for me.

A thin youngish white man came towards me from out of the shadows of the police station's long corridor, looking at me. He smirked and asked me, "Don't you remember me? I met you at the police station a few weeks ago."

I replied in the negative.

It appeared as though the man was enjoying my predicament and was trying to rub his presence in, even though it was not relevant to the situation.

Before undergoing the fairly humiliating process of confiscation of property, search, and the removal of my belt, I was questioned at length by Sgt Jones and his colleague, who kept glaring at me as though I were the absolute scum of the world. Jones explained that they regarded me as an "international conman," who had been applying for jobs with various police forces in Britain, and that none of the statements I'd made on the application forms or in my CV could be verified by his "enquiry officers," who had prepared "reports" against me as a result. He claimed that they had been after me for quite some time and had finally caught up with me and that I was to be questioned under caution. It appeared that an all-points bulletin in true FBI-style had been published against me!

After spending nearly an hour with these two men, I was finally charged with deception, searched, read my rights, and locked up in a small cell that was quite cold and not well lit there in the police station. By this time I was still a bit confused and in an attempt to have at least another witness to verify what had gone on at the police station, I requested a solicitor. I was allowed to make a phone call, and the only person I could think of calling was the solicitor at the Citizen Advice Bureau who was handling my immigration matter. I tried to contact her but learnt that the office had closed for the day and that I would have to call her in the morning. I then requested a duty solicitor who dealt with police matters. I was hesitant to speak to these two British policemen until I had legal assistance. Someone from the front desk looked into finding me a duty solicitor, and my interrogators told me to wait until the department had secured something.

I waited in the concrete cell, which was getting colder by the hour. My request for paper and a pen was not agreed to by the guard patrolling outside my cell. The lighting got poorer as it began to get dark. I was offered a cup of tea and, somewhat later during the day, a container containing sparsely cooked lasagne. After what looked like ages, during which I felt a big pain in the rear of my head and a rise in my blood pressure, I was finally relieved to see the key turning in the door and the tall sergeant on duty telling me that I was going to be interrogated by Jones and Colbeck. The duty solicitor had finally shown up. I had been locked up in that cell (something that had never happened before in my life) for over four hours.

The duty solicitor (a young man from a local solicitor's office) explained to me that the so-called criminal charges against me were the supposed use of deception or attempted deception by lying in my application forms and CV while applying for the jobs with the British Police forces. I expressed my shock and outrage to him and asked him to express my feelings to the interrogating officers. This made little difference, as I was soon ushered into a chamber and was informed that I was being interrogated under caution and that the entire proceedings were being recorded and would be used against me if required.

What followed will be etched in my memory for life. I was asked lots of overtly stupid questions, which were allegations pertaining to my academic life, my arrival in Britain, and my career with the Pakistan police. These characters accepted none of the statements I'd written in either my CV or the application forms. Colbeck glared at me silently, while Jones posed the questions, one after the other, rolling his eyes every time I gave a reply. I rebutted all the allegations; the so-called interrogation really looked like a ping-pong match, with the ball going from one side to the other – allegation, rebuttal, allegation, rebuttal, and so on. Colbeck interposed only once to ask me if I had used any other names to apply to jobs, to which I replied in the negative. It seemed like an absurd question, and I couldn't help thinking if he asked this of all applicants or had only reserved the inane question for me.

I denied all of the officers' allegations in their entirety and offered to show them documentary evidence to verify all that I'd stated in the CV and on the application form. After what seemed like ages, they finally agreed and the interview was terminated. I was then taken, while under their custody, to my living quarters in Roath, where I showed them documents in the shape of certificates, testimonials, and references from various people to verify that all was true. After another one-hour interrogation in my room, I was again taken back to the police station and was told that the officers were temporarily satisfied and that I was going to be bailed out but would be asked to return to answer bail at a later time.

I was given a paper stating that I was being released on bail and giving the date and location of my expected return to answer bail. I was finally given my belongings and was free to leave. As I exited the police station, my head was swinging and all sorts of thoughts were coming into my mind. I looked at my watch and realised that I had spent more than eight hours in this drama. I swore to myself that I would make these British policemen pay for what they had made me go through that day.

Two

Background

I was born and raised in the city of Karachi, the second child and son of five children. My father was an officer in the government who had served in India before 1947 and had then opted for Pakistan at partition. My paternal family hailed from a "Muslim majority" district of Muzaffarnagar in northern India, located about 100 miles north of Delhi. My mother was a head teacher of a girls' school in Delhi. I spent most of my early life in a medium-sized home in a middle class suburb of Karachi. We kids all went to a well-reputed private school in the city.

During my conversations with my father, he related to me fairly vivid details of the partition of the subcontinent in 1947, which he had witnessed first-hand. Specifically, I remember him telling me about the mass exodus of refugees from both sides of the border and how he used to board trains from Lahore to cross the border into India (as required by his service with the government). The trains arrived from India with corpses of Muslim migrants who had been cut to pieces by sword-brandishing Hindu and Sikh extremists opposed to their departure and to the division of the country. The trains used to be washed clean and then returned to India with the passengers, which included my father. He also witnessed rotting corpses and carcasses lying on both sides of the train lines during his journeys. He never once expressed any fear of these trips as a result. These experiences taught me to be fearless in life.

I enjoyed an above average academic record at school and was frequently the favourite of most of the teachers. Due to some good fortune and higher grades in mathematics and sciences, I secured admission and a scholarship to the Massachusetts Institute of Technology in the USA, earning the admiration of most of my colleagues during the last years of school. I joined in late 1975, choosing to study engineering. Upon first arriving in the West, I experienced a big cultural change, which took me some time to adjust to. During my four years at the institute, I took several courses in economics and social sciences and found that I could also obtain a second major in economics with only two more courses. I duly finished these and had the opportunity of cross registering for three courses with nearby Harvard University's Department of Economics.

I left MIT in late 1979 but wasn't able to get the graduation certificate until two years later due to an incomplete undergraduate thesis. I worked for a consulting company in Washington DC for a few months before returning to Karachi in early 1982. Here I sat for the Government's Central Superior Services Examination and secured a high position. I was subsequently allocated to the Police Service. I served in various capacities in the federal and provincial police forces in Pakistan in the Sindh and Punjab provinces. I also served for one year in the Frontier Constabulary in the tribal area of South Waziristan.

In February 1984, I married (as an arranged affair) the daughter of a retired army officer. My elder daughter was born in September 1987 and the younger one in January 1989.

I had differences with my wife, and this was compounded by excessive interference by her parents and sisters, who did not appear at all enlightened. She, being British born, had obtained without my knowledge or consent, a British passport for herself while on a trip for medical treatment in the UK in 1997. She used this to obtain passports for the two girls and, in a bizarre and sudden move, left for the UK in May 1998 with the girls to supposedly "settle" there on a permanent basis. Prior to moving to the UK she, with the support of her parents and her sisters, had filed lawsuits through solicitors in the Karachi court for permanent custody of the children. She filed these a day before she departed for London. I was later informed by solicitors in the UK that this amounted to "international abduction" of minor children by one parent, a fairly common occurrence in this part of the world.

I conceived of her actions as being based on her great desire to move permanently to the UK, as well as on quite poor and perverse advice given to her by her parents, members of her family, and her legal advisor, a London qualified barrister. My father-in-law was a retired Colonel from the Pakistan Army, and my mother-in-law was head teacher of a private school in Karachi. I expected better guidance and better advice from people of such background, if only to keep their daughter from ruining her married life and seriously affecting the lives of my daughters. But outward appearances and estimates of human character can be quite wrong, as I learnt to my dismay.

I followed up the proceedings that my wife had initiated in the Karachi court and got these dismissed within a few months. I knew that my eventual trip to Britain to bring my daughters back to Pakistan would be difficult, as I would have to go through the legal process in that country and English family laws were known to be hugely biased in favour of mothers. I felt that having relevant court orders from Pakistan would, nevertheless, help me in my plight. I therefore filed a counteraction for custody of the children. Due to the unreasonable behaviour of the mother, who was held by the court in its judgement to have filed the suits simply to harass me, I was given the custody orders that I had filed for. These were issued to me in March 1999, and on receipt, I immediately applied for a visit visa to the UK at the British High Commission in Karachi.

I arrived at the High Commission in late March 1999 at Runnymede Lane in Clifton, Karachi, and was told to wait in the waiting area. My application for a visa had been recommended by the Pakistan Foreign Office in Karachi. However, I was later informed in an interview with the visa officer that there was a problem in issuing me the visa but that, as he put it, "The High Commission would not come into any matrimonial conflict between you and your wife." At that time I was unable to understand what this implied. Only about two years later in Cardiff was I to able to see in writing, through my solicitor, the application that my estranged wife had submitted through her lawyer to the High Commission in Karachi, asking them not to issue me with any visa at all as I would then use this to travel to Britain and try to take the girls back to Pakistan. This was the real reason for the difficulty I faced in obtaining the visa. I may add here that I had, in fact, visited Britain on two prior occasions, the visit visas being issued to me by the same authority without any cross-examination.

I was a full-time employee of the Pakistani government and was, at that time, posted in the Intelligence Bureau in Karachi. The department was well aware of my matrimonial problems and readily agreed to grant me the leave, initially for thirty days to be extended to sixty days on my request. It is important to point out here that, from what I later learnt in Britain, one and possibly two of my own seniors in the department had aided and facilitated my wife in her clandestine and premeditated flight to Britain. I exchanged terse words with them as a result and decided that I could not continue working with these people any further.

I arrived in Britain in mid-April 1999 with nothing more than a suitcase of personal belongings and US$1000 in my possession. But I had with me, of course, records of all the proceedings and judgements from the Karachi Court and fully expected the authorities here to help me search for the children and assist me in taking them back to their country of natural residence. My visit to the UK was urged on by the British Home Office who, on contact via email, had advised me that the office could not give me any details of the whereabouts and welfare of my daughters, as they were British subjects, and that I would have to come to the UK and contact a solicitor.

My wife, with the full assistance and connivance of her sister in South Wales and her parents in Karachi, had been constantly deceiving me as to the whereabouts and welfare of my daughters. I was given no address or telephone number for them and was merely told by these people in unison that they were "in London". I never believed a word of it and, through my own efforts in Karachi, had actually traced a telephone number in Cardiff, which I suspected to be the children's. On arrival in London, I contacted the Pakistan High Commission in Lowndes Square and asked for their cooperation in the matter. The High Commission introduced me to a gentleman who was based in Cardiff and agreed to assist me in that city. I stayed in the Pakistan consulate's hostel in London for two days and then made my way to Cardiff.

I found Cardiff to be quite a picturesque city. But I had little time for sightseeing, given the things on my mind. I was lucky to find a room with a Pakistani friend (who, incidentally, also hailed from Karachi) and initiated proceedings through a prominent solicitor, John Doel, in Cardiff. Through entirely my own efforts, I had succeeded in locating the whereabouts of the children. A hearing was held in the district court in Cardiff but was then moved to the High Court in London due to the international aspect of the matter. The Judge, Mr R. Connell, passed a judgement that my solicitor and I had least expected. Despite the illegal behaviour of the mother and the difficulties I had faced in first locating the children and then in instituting proceedings, he smirked directly at me and ordered that the children would stay on in Britain, while accepting that Pakistan was their country of natural residence. I found his order to be quite unpalatable, almost offensive, and it looked almost certain to me that he was slighting the Pakistan legal system and the laws of that country. He called for another slightly bigger hearing the next month (June 1999) but with the same outcome. I felt, as did Mr Doel, that the Judge had leaned too far in what he conceived to be the welfare of the children in the United Kingdom while negating everything that stood in opposition to that conclusion, including the mother's criminal behaviour and that the children's country of birth and natural residence was Pakistan and not the United Kingdom. He seemed to question and belittle unfairly the family laws of Pakistan, which I felt he was not competent to do. We felt that this, in and of itself, constituted a legal error fit for appeal, but I decided to acquiesce and not go further, as the litigation was having a damaging effect on the children.

I felt humiliated by what this Judge had done The judgment of the British Judge was partly in line with what a colleague of mine in Karachi (a British-qualified barrister) had informed me, namely that the British family courts heavily favoured mothers (as against the rights of fathers) and that I would face a difficult task in convincing any British judge of my strong grounds for taking the children back to Pakistan, including the Pakistan court judgments which were in my favour. What compounded the matter, to my dismay, was the totally perfunctory and deceptive evidence given by the mother, her two sisters, and her niece who had shown up for the hearings.

I felt strongly about filing an appeal based on the judge's obvious factual and legal errors in leaning too far with the welfare principle but then felt that the girls were already under huge pressure and did not want to return to Pakistan. Further, their mother had instilled in them great feelings of insecurity, primarily because I was with the Karachi Police at the time and supposedly had "connections" by which I could prevent them from ever returning to Britain. They were firm in their desire to stay in Britain, and after consultation with my brother and mother, I decided that it would not be appropriate to file an appeal. Legal aid for such an appeal had been denied as advice from Counsel was in the negative. Under the British legal system, if advice from the barrister (referred to as Counsel) is against the chances of success at appeal, the Legal Services Commission does not grant legal aid for preparing and filing such appeal in the Court of Appeal. As such, I was forced to acquiesce to my daughters continued stay in the country, even though everything in me desired the opposite. I knew that a prolonged exposure for them at such ages to a Western system would negatively affect them, and I did not desire such an effect at all. Besides, my contact with them would, at best, be superficial. Later events were to prove me correct in more ways than one.

Three

The Employment Applications

My decision not to return to Pakistan, despite my employer's (the Pakistani Government's) warnings that it would initiate disciplinary action, involved some determination and hard work. I was a frequent visitor to the Cardiff Council's Enterprise Centre on City Road and was now more than ever helped by the staff there to prepare my CV for the oncoming job applications that I needed to make in attempts to find a suitable job. Three CVs were prepared, one for applications as a police officer of some capacity, one as a business manager, and a third as a teacher – the last because I had had significant teaching experience in Karachi. I went through the listings with Jobcentres and with the Enterprise Centre almost on a daily basis while living in Roath.

My prime interest was to find a job in any police force here in Britain, as I'd worked for more than thirteen years with a similar force in Pakistan. As a result, I frequently perused the classified section of the *Police Review* that I found at the main public library in Cardiff. I hoped to find an opening for a position with a decision-making capacity in the police force. As my last posting had been with the Intelligence Bureau in Islamabad, I felt that the position of intelligence Analyst would be suited well to me. The work of an intelligence analyst with the British police was very similar to the work I'd been doing during the preceding years. I made an initial application to Kent Police in about April 2000 for a similar vacancy in their Maidstone headquarters. I was elated to hear back from the Kent Police Personnel Department shortly thereafter, asking me to come in for a day of interviews and testing. I was to be partly reimbursed for my travelling expenses and would be allowed to stay overnight in the training quarters at no cost to me. I decided to make the trip.

I reported to reception at the police HQ and was duly given a key for the bachelor accommodation. The psychometric testing, scenario analysis and interviews were held the following day. I noted, with not too much concern, that the other interviewees were all "white" and I was, as such, the only "minority" candidate for the post. I was later to learn that interviews were held for about seventeen candidates in all over two days and that all the remaining candidates were white and British. My interview was held by a panel of three people, one of whom I later learnt was Richard Anderson, the Head of the Intelligence Wing of Kent Police.

I left by train to return to Cardiff later in the afternoon. I was not too surprised to hear back from the Personnel Department of Kent Police within two days, stating that "although you came a close second", the post had been given to someone else. This statement would be hotly contested by the Kent Police during the litigation, who later took the view that I had not been a "close second" to the post and that my claim to this extent was flawed. They also later wrote to me asking that I return the room key, which I had forgotten to hand over at the time of my departure. I duly returned the key to the Personnel Department.

Somewhat disappointed that I'd not received the position, I soon tried to forget about it and went on submitting other applications. I applied for a similar job with the South Wales Police, which the force had advertised with Job Centres, as well as with the Enterprise Centre. I sent my application as required sometime in the middle of June 2000. I received no reply, not even an acknowledgement. I made one phone call to the South Wales Police Personnel Department to inquire about the outcome but was not given any positive reply or even an acknowledgement of my application. There was nothing further I could do.

I made a further application to the Kent Police for a similar post that was also advertised in *Police Review* a few weeks later. I sent in an application along with a copy of the same CV that I had sent for the earlier application.

On both application forms, I had written in bold capitals the words, "PLEASE SEE CV ATTACHED." I was later to learn that the decision-makers at the receiving end had totally ignored this request.

I may state here that I'd had a fairly sporadic interaction with South Wales Police during my stay in Cardiff, which was for well over a year prior to the job applications. The local officers had known me quite well and had seen me around. In particular, I remember speaking to the young constable who later tried to speak mockingly to me during the encounter with Sgt Jones, DC Colbeck, and their colleagues at the Rumney Police Station a year later. I recall filing a report for the theft of my car, which had been stolen from outside my home in Roath during the early part of 2000. I later learnt from a source that the police were actually bent on accusing me of insurance fraud on this count, taking me (totally falsely again) to have engineered the theft of this car and then to have it set alight so that I could make a deceptive insurance claim. The idea was quite preposterous, and I felt extremely insulted when I heard about it. The car was later recovered (without damage) and my elimination prints were taken, ostensibly to clear me of charges of deception and a bogus insurance claim.

I subsequently had made other job applications to the Essex Police, Grampian Police, and Tayside Police (in Scotland) and had received acknowledgements and offers of interviews from the various forces. The posts were advertised in *Police Review*. Each interview was held in the respective headquarters, but I would later learn that I had been sidelined without reason. No constructive feedback was offered to me, even on inquiry.

In September 2000 I received an invitation to a "Meet the Beat" event from the Avon and Somerset Constabulary in Portishead, Bristol. This event was to be held at the Jury's Inn in Bristol and was to run for the whole day. I was not informed at that time that it was specifically meant for minorities. I attended this event and met the Chief Constable as well

15

as the heads of the other wings of the Police Force at that time. I also remember well meeting the Head of Personnel, a woman named Linda Pope. Linda Pope encouraged me to apply for a currently vacant post of intelligence analyst with the police force. I did as she'd asked and sent in my CV after returning to Cardiff. The CV was the same one I'd sent to all the other police forces. I did not receive any acknowledgement of receipt of my application or an offer of an interview.

This was the last job application I made to the police forces in Britain. It was now the beginning of November, and I waited for any further response from any one of them. I heard nothing on any of these applications, until 9 January 2001 when I was contacted by Ali to inform me that two police officers from the Avon and Somerset Police wanted to speak to me about a job application I had made with them.

Four

The Claim

The very next day after being released on bail, I made few phone calls and was advised to contact both the Cardiff Law Centre located in Roath and Race Equality First located in the town centre. I secured an appointment with a solicitor at the law centre and with the caseworker at Race Equality First. After consultation with both, I was advised that my discrimination claim against all three police forces was stronger than that of wrongful arrest and confinement and that I should pursue the claim in the discrimination tribunal. Accordingly, on advice, I filed a joint claim for employment discrimination in the Cardiff Tribunals in March 2001 against the Chief Constables of Kent County Constabulary, the South Wales Police, and the Avon and Somerset Constabulary in Portishead, Bristol.

After an initial hearing in Cardiff, the matter was referred to the Ashford Tribunals in Kent, as the discrimination was deemed to have been initiated by the Kent Police, headquartered in Maidstone. The case against the South Wales Police was to be heard in Cardiff, while that against the Avon and Somerset Police was also sent to Ashford.

In Cardiff, the judgement went against me as we were deemed to be out of time in filing a legal form known as the ET1 or the claim notice. This had to be filed within ninety days of the alleged discrimination under the stipulations of UK's Race Relations Act, 1975. The Tribunal held, unanimously, that time was to be counted from the date of my job application with the South Wales Police and not from the date of my arrest. I may clarify here that it was only on my arrest on 10 January 2001 that I learnt that I was being looked upon as a criminal and was not considered to be a job applicant at all. The Tribunal, despite our protestations, felt otherwise. My Solicitor and I appealed to the Employment Appeal Tribunal. The EAT sent the case back to the Cardiff Tribunals for a rehearing based on the same facts.

In a wholly biased hearing, about which I later filed a complaint with the President of the Tribunals, the decision again was that we were out of time and the matter could not, as a result, proceed to a full hearing. I may state here that Cardiff tribunals are fairly well known for the perverse decisions they give out (as I learnt later). And these two decisions, coming in tandem, made them live up well to their reputation. I never received a reply to my complaint. I felt bitter, as I knew well (and this was later confirmed) that most of the initial groundwork for their actions had been carried out by the South Wales Police. Tribunals have the full discretion to extend time beyond 90 day time limit set down under the Race Relations Act. In the subject case, my lack of knowledge of any criminal action being planned against me by the South Wales Police and the great damage caused to me due to their illegal acts should have been sufficient reason for this Tribunal to so relax the time stipulations, which was no more than a few months. I was a resident in the jurisdiction of the South Wales Police force and interactions with them (including the so-called inquiries) had been taking place in Cardiff for almost the entire year prior to the arrest. The South Wales Police had thus been allowed to go without answering for the wanton discriminatory acts carried out by several members of its force. I don't believe I will ever forget the performance of that part-time Chairman or her unenlightened colleagues that day.

The matter against the Kent Police and Avon and Somerset Police was heard in Ashford, Kent. Based primarily on the same facts that my Solicitor had presented to the Cardiff Tribunal, the Ashford Tribunal decided that my case would proceed to a full hearing, even though the time after filing the job application for this case was about three months longer than for those against the other two police forces. It was decided in a later hearing that the matter against the Avon and Somerset Police should be heard in the Bristol Tribunals.

At the hearing in the Bristol Tribunals in April 2004, the judgement was not in my favour, even though the Tribunal stated that the "reports" prepared against me were profoundly flawed. In fact, except for stating my name and date of birth correctly, these so-called reports were the most confounded pieces of writing compiled by anyone, and the compiler happened to be a Detective Constable of the South Wales Police! I saw the same two faces of the arresting officers I had seen in Rumney Police Station more than three years prior. The Bristol Judgement itself was quite perverse and reeked of bias by the Tribunal. I sent an immediate review petition, but the Tribunal turned it down.

My faith in the British Tribunals at this time was at the lowest that it had ever been, given my encounters in Cardiff. I felt that the tribunals had abused their discretion in order to protect their own kind, while at the same time accepting that the treatment the police forces had meted out to me was totally unjustified and based on falsification of facts. I felt that a white tribunal could never find one of their own kind guilty of anything, even in the light of the most damning evidence. I was the only "minority" or coloured candidate out of seventeen that had applied for the job, and only I was picked out arbitrarily and accused of deception. I had not deceived one iota and was taken to be guilty on all counts, and the concerned policemen had carried out the arrest and interrogation without carrying out even the minimal of investigations. Why did they make the accusations in the first place? Was this a standard policy in vetting the applications by any of these police forces? Clearly this was not the case, as none of the others had been subjected to this treatment or to anything close to it, even though they may well have been deceiving and lying on their CVs and application forms.

Under the laws of discrimination in the country, the claimant has to firstly show that he or she is, or hails from, a "minority" (as against a white British comparator). My solicitor showed the tribunals that I was a minority, and the latter accepted this as fact. The claimant then has to show that he or she received treatment that was different, discriminatory, less, more offensive, or more malicious than that meted out to the comparator. My solicitor and I also clearly showed this to be the case. Once a claimant establishes these two premises, the onus or burden of proof shifts to the employer or the respondent, who then has to show rational cause or justification as to why such treatment was meted out to the claimant. If the respondent is unable to justify the treatment conclusively (or, as in this case, show it to be a matter of standard procedure) the claim is held to be proven and goes to remedy. Why couldn't the Cardiff and Bristol tribunals see all this and find what the Ashford tribunals would finally find? I can only point to the composition and the location of the former two tribunals that led to miscarriages of justice.

According to present-day discrimination specialists and psychologists, the vast majority of discrimination cases all over the Western world are based on subconscious, as opposed to conscious, discrimination. This was a classic case of subconscious discrimination, as none of these policemen (numbering more than twelve and all white "majority" Britons) had ever mentioned that I was to be treated differently because I was Asian or of Pakistani origin or a Muslim. In fact, they gave no reason as to why I was treated differently. Because the policemen could offer no explanation to justify their treatment, the tribunals should have found the accusation of race discrimination to be true under British anti-discrimination laws, and my claim should have been upheld. But they were not by both the Cardiff and Bristol Tribunals. I felt saddened by the treatment meted out to me by the police forces and then by the tribunals that had treated the claim with the scantest of respect and feeling. In Pakistan, I had all along held British police and the judiciary in high esteem. However, my exposure to both these law enforcing arms left this respect in tatters. I was at a loss and didn't know how to approach the matter further.

I felt totally frustrated on receipt of the judgement. As a result, I decided henceforth to have a go at the perpetrators myself and relieved the legal advisors of their duties. At this time, I also could not afford legal advisors. I had been teaching Advanced Level (A-Level) mathematics and economics

in a sixth form college in Cardiff and had later taught maths at a boys'
school in Fulham, London. I was currently privately tutoring in these same
subjects and made just about enough money to keep me going. I decided,
therefore, to appear in person for the last hearing in the Ashford Tribunals
in July 2005.

Five

The Hearing

The hearing, scheduled for five days, lasted actually for four days, with Ms Christiana Hyde as the Chairperson and Mr M. Gallager and Mr Blackwell as the two other lay members. I and the Chairperson (a Black lady with, as I was to learn later, an excellent reputation) carried out a thorough cross-examination of the three witnesses the defence presented to us. These were Richard Anderson, the Head of the Kent Police Intelligence Wing; DC Clive Russell, investigation officer on behalf of Kent Police; and DC C. White, the investigation officer on behalf of South Wales Police. The two arresting officers from the Avon and Somerset Police failed to show up for the hearing, but their earlier statements were attached to the evidence.

The three witnesses were broken down bit by bit and were exposed to be, in fact, deceiving and lying in their statements, with not even one of their allegations based on reason and factual inquiry but totally on fabrications, prevarications, and concoctions bordering on perversity. They were unable to justify, to any degree, even one of their actions, writings, or thoughts about me. I must express admiration for the Chairperson in particular, who carried out the bulk of the questioning herself and took an active interest in the proceedings. The three witnesses had no answer when the Chairperson posed the crucial question – why had they not set their treatment of me as standard procedure for all applicants and treated each applicant similarly? In addition, they were unable to produce a single piece of evidence to back up their allegations of lies and deception on my part or to prove that they'd made any contact with the organisations mentioned in my CV.

The head of the Intelligence Wing of Kent Police, Richard Anderson, in particular (the main brains behind the entire drama) came out quite poorly during cross-examination. His body language was particularly revealing. He shivered and shook, drank several glasses of water, and avoided any eye contact with me. He also forgot to sign his name, even when asked by the Chairperson to do so. He was pathetically unable to justify any of his allegations or to offer any rational basis for holding me supposedly fit for "criminal sanction", as he put it. He looked like a completely cornered individual who had realised belatedly that he had made a big mess and was in much trouble as a result. The questions were coming and, despite his best efforts, he had no satisfactory answers. His colleague was a grossly overweight detective constable named Clive Russell, with a huge beer belly and twenty-three years of police work behind him (as he claimed). He was the other idiot who was responsible for spreading the gospel to the other police forces, perhaps through his own version of an all-points bulletin! He was also the "investigating officer" from Kent Police. Based on his perfunctory inquiries, I did not feel that he deserved this title. I was unable to see him fit for any police force based perhaps only on his physique. I was appalled to see how the Kent Police had been able to put up with an incompetent, incomprehensible buffoon like him for all this time. He was unable to present any evidence or even any records of his "investigations" into his allegations whatsoever. Neither of them was able to answer as to why they were looking for first or further degrees from me when the stated qualification requirements for the post were just two A-Levels. The deeds and mindsets of these two men in this matter reeked of pure wickedness.

It is worth mentioning here that both these individuals did not even possess A Level qualifications having received, by their own admission, a few GCSE passes with average grades. Neither of them was able to offer any explanation as to why he had not tried to contact me at any time via telephone to clarify the matter, when the exact same number was stated in bold digits on both the application forms. It was quite evident that there never was any desire on both of them (or any of the other Investigating Officers) to resolve the matter and to give me a fair chance to explain what they felt needed clarification.

DC Ken Colbeck, the principal investigating officer from the Avon and Somerset Police force, did not show up for the hearing. Despite my efforts, I did not get a chance to break him down. His statement was attached, and I would really have liked to cross-examine him and have a go at *his* so-called investigations and "reports". I had seen him in Bristol, but my advisor had not cross-examined him to the degree that he should have. Colbeck had supposedly made contact with an individual from the Northumbria Police force (where I had completed a training course) and had added more false and outrageous allegations against me as a result of his conversations with that person. I felt that Colbeck was the other clown who had unfairly escaped cross-examination and culpability during the hearing.

It is also worth pointing out that with the Kent Police, as with the other two accused police forces, a supervisory officer with the title of detective superintendent was, in effect, supervising the entire proceedings of the staff. I was quite amazed to note that none of these so-called supervisory officers, with several decades of qualified policing experience behind them, had actually done any policing at all as far as this matter was concerned. Their supervision lacked any substance whatsoever, and rather than pulling up those directly under their command for their perfunctory and flawed inquiries, the supervisors actually endorsed these very inquiries and instigated their juniors to proceed with the criminal prosecution. They could easily have stemmed the rot had they, at any time during this episode, demanded or directed their so-called inquiry officers to obtain positive, documentary evidence of even one of their allegations of "deception". The performance of everyone in the police force who was involved with the incident reeked of gross incompetence and institutionalised racism all the way up.

While my protracted cross-examinations of the main witnesses left me with a quickly dwindling respect for the British police forces in general, I learned that the performance of their legal advisors, particularly that for the Kent Police, was even more pathetic. This matter was what I would regard to be a simple case or, as some would say it, an open and shut case of race discrimination. Only I among over seventeen candidates had been taken to be a deceitful criminal and was subsequently arrested, charged, and interrogated under caution when none of the allegations were true to any degree. None of the other candidates had been so treated. Further this was at worst for me and at best for these police forces, a case of attempted deception, in which I had only submitted an application for employment that had upset them so much. I had never been employed or had earned a single penny by the so-called deception. So why had they taken the matter to such an extent?

It always appeared to me as though the officers involved were enraged that a displaced "Paki" would dare apply for a job meant for one of their own and felt strongly that the fit punishment for me for the outrage was to be arrested, charged, locked up and interrogated under caution, upon which I was expected to forthwith cough up the truth (as they saw it). It was, to me and to my legal advisors, a serious and most unprecedented case of race discrimination by these police forces. Now that I had been supposedly bailed out and the bail was confirmed and all charges were later dropped, why could the legal advisors, seeing all this in correct perspective and with the advantage of hindsight, not have arrived at this conclusion within a few weeks at most of initiation of proceedings? I was unable to understand this, as none of the three forces had ever offered any reconciliation or compensation or even a word of remorse or regret for their actions. They were quite arrogant in defence of their nonsensical actions and reports to the very last, arguing and fighting quite stupidly in trying to justify and rationalise what simply could not be justified or rationalised. But more crucially their legal advisors, well-reputed barristers and solicitors all round, were consistently giving them poor and perverse advice by making them keep on fighting when the only sober, mature, and correct course of action was to offer apologies and some meaningful compensation for the damages caused and to essentially call it a day with a handshake. At least one of these Barristers was also a sitting part-time Chairman of a Tribunal.

Perhaps the advisors were attempting to prolong the legal battle in order to clock more time and essentially earn more money. I brought out this point in my submissions to the Ashford Tribunal. The Kent Police Counsel (Ms Sophie Garner), supposedly a discrimination specialist, looked and performed like an absolute idiot in the court. I felt that her performance was not much better than a badly behaved child in a primary school class, and she was almost told off in such manner by the Chairperson. It would have been more appropriate if Ms Garner had been made to stand in the corner as punishment! I was left wondering how she had been admitted to the Bar in the first place. Possibly, it was an error of judgement or else the Bar Council itself needed to be pulled up to make its procedures more stringent.

To give an example of her line of defence, Ms Garner tried (completely unsuccessfully) to use the issue of my immigration status in the country to justify discrimination, claiming that I was not given permission to work in the UK and thus could not even apply for a job in this country. She tried desperately to hammer that point during the main hearing and then again in her review petition and the remedy hearing. While there *is* a bar against being gainfully employed while on a visit visa (which I had), there is absolutely no bar under the immigration rules for anyone to *look for* or *apply* to any job even on that category of visa. Further, her clients had never established my visa situation at the time of application or even thereafter, either in the application form or at the interview or even by mail. So why this desperate attempt to justify her client's activities after five years of litigation?

Ms Garner's arguments looked more like a sinking ship trying desperately to cling to imaginary straws. The advisor would have been wiser to have advised her clients to file proceedings in the Asylum and Immigration Tribunals under the immigration laws rather than to use this line in the Employment Tribunal. Was it the wrong Tribunal, though, or was it the

wrong Counsel and poor advice? It was a perverse line of defence, and the Tribunal readily saw it as such and threw it out in its entirety. It did not find even a simple mention in the judgement. The visa question would have been somewhat relevant had the Kent Police thought of employing me or made me an offer or if I had ever been employed by them and had concealed the visa situation.

The lady's performance in the court also gave away a fairly crucial line in their defence, namely that these three police forces may have been fighting in separate tribunals but they were actually one as far as I was concerned. She used the same arguments that the Counsel for the Avon and Somerset Police had used in the Bristol hearing and even tried to use the very same legal authorities that had been used by them. It didn't work this time around. The Ashford Tribunal threw out all these arguments and authorities. The Kent Police Counsel knew of the outcome of the other proceedings even before I got to know of it. For instance, Miss Garner knew (and stated as such to the Tribunal) that my review petition before the Bristol Tribunal had been set aside, even though this had only happened the day before and I had not even received confirmation to the effect.

If connivance and abetment between these police forces was a means of building up their "criminal" charges against me, this continued unabated, even after proceedings had been initiated and during the litigation. As a result, I felt the full brunt of the forces' institutional racism; with determination and arrogance, each force gave succour to each other rather than seeing the matter rationally and from a broader perspective. At no time during my five years of litigation against these police forces did any of the parties involved or their legal advisors try to see and feel things from my point of view. This failure to look at the specifics of the case in favour of protecting their own highlights the collective arrogance that guides the actions of the British police forces and renders these forces a great danger to minorities in Britain. I could imagine what they must have done to others who had similarly accused them of racism.

Six

The Judgements

The Ashford judgement was delivered after a delay of over three months, on 31 October 2005. It was based on twenty-two pages of text (comprising 100 paragraphs). My claim was upheld on four counts, including, crucially, the charge of aiding and abetting discrimination by the Kent Police, a charge that is unique to British employment law. The counts which were not upheld were due only to what I believe to be wholly biased judgements of the Cardiff and Bristol Tribunals, which had not found in my favour. Aiding and abetting discrimination was also an allegation my solicitor had belatedly added to the claim, and while the abettor of discrimination (Kent Police) had been found to have aided and abetted the discrimination, the two abetters had not been found guilty of the tort. As such, the counts involving these two police forces had not been upheld.

All the defendants' assertions, principally the belated charge of my immigration status and visa, were thrown out. Kent Police had never, at any time during the interview and evaluation or even shortly thereafter, determined from me the nature of my immigration status in the United Kingdom, so why their legal team had picked up this issue after nearly five years of litigation was a question that remained unresolved. The Tribunal did not deign to even give this a simple mention in its Judgement. The main Judgment was quite critical of all the major players from amongst the three police forces who were involved in this nonsense. Totally they numbered at least twelve, and all were white and British. It essentially boiled down to my word against the combined word of all these people, and, based on the evidence, I was taken to be truthful and all of them were taken to be lying and deceiving. On a balance of probabilities, as stated by the Tribunal, I was also taken to be truthful in my assertion that I had been informed that I had come a close second in the first job interview.

The charges made against me by these people were, in effect, reversed and were applied to them in turn.

The remedy hearing, held on the 15 December 2005, lasted for a whole day. I was fortunate to be assisted by Ms Lisa Connerty, a Solicitor for the Croydon Law Centre who was acting as a McKenzie's friend. I may clarify here that a McKenzie's friend assists a litigant in person in a common law court. He or she does not need to be legally qualified, the point being that litigants in person are entitled to have assistance in their case, either by lay or professional persons. I also learnt that a review petition filed by the defendants on the Judgement had been set aside by the Tribunal. There was no appeal, however, and the respondents finally accepted the Judgement as legal.

I may state here that, in the middle of 2003 (more than two years after the arrest of January 2001) I submitted job applications to several schools for mathematics teaching posts. As my career with the police had to come to an abrupt end, I decided to try to change my career path and pursue teaching. I'd had teaching experience in Karachi and had also served in a semi teaching capacity with the Pakistan police as Head of a Police Training Academy in Karachi. I did not receive a reply or a satisfactory reply from almost all of the schools to which I applied. I felt that the educational institutions were taking a view of me that was similar to that of the police forces, and were preparing charges similar to those that the police forces had advanced against me.

When I'd first filed my discrimination suit against the police forces, the first tribunal that looked at my case had ruled that I was time barred, as it had been more than ninety days since I'd applied for the jobs in question and when the discrimination alleged had taken place. I did not want this to happen again, and solely with this objective in mind, approached solicitors for advice. Based entirely on this advice and all through solicitors, Section 65 Race Relations Act questionnaires were sent to these schools (numbering over forty) seeking answers that had not been made through written requests for feedback. With this, claims had to be filed as stipulated by the law. There was no law by virtue of which the reasons for rejection could be determined, and solicitors had no powers to elicit a response from the schools through letters written on letterhead. Besides, legal aid did not cover writing letters as a part of litigation.

Shortly after the claims were filed, I received a sudden visit from an individual who claimed to be a reporter from *The Evening Standard*. He started asking me questions about these claims. I partly answered them but then referred him to the solicitor who was acting on my behalf. I did not realise then that his colleague sitting in a nearby car was busy photographing me. I was shocked to see my picture on page three of *The Evening Standard* the next week, along with the headline "Asian Teacher Rejected by over 40 Schools Sues All of Them". While this was not exactly true, several other major newspapers in London (including the *Daily Mail*, *The Independent*, and *The Times* of London) carried this story in their columns during the coming days. I had become a superstar of sorts and didn't like it at all. As I was to find out later, this focus on me led to the dissemination of various sorts of virtually slanderous comments by people (including chairmen of more than one tribunal) against me. They accused me of filing these "claims" for the purpose of extorting money. These comments were highly insulting and offensive and did not have one iota of truth in them.

This issue was picked up by the Kent Police legal team, whose legal advisor wrote to her counsel in efforts to use it against me and to have me declared as a serial litigant. The schools matter came three years after I'd filed the claim against the Kent Police and could not, in any conceivable way, have any retrospective impact on the police matter. A copy of the legal team's communication fell into my hands, and I put this up to the Court to show the aggravating behaviour of the Kent Police legal team. The Tribunal took notice of the respondents' activities and promised to award me aggravated damages as a result. In its thirteen-page Remedy Judgement dated 28

March 2006, the Tribunal awarded me a total of £65,746.73 in damages, including £25,000 for injury to feelings (one of the highest under the Vento bands) £4,000 for aggravated damages, and £5,000 exemplary damages (as part of punitive damages). The Tribunal had awarded the latter to as it considered the total absence of any apology or effort to settle by the Kent Police for over four years as aggravating enough. The rest of the award consisted of loss of earnings, future loss of earnings, and interest. The Chief Constable of Kent Police was also ordered to apologise in writing to me for the actions of his force members.

In mid-March 2006 I received a cheque from Kent Police for the awarded amount, along with a letter of apology from the Chief Constable dated 8 February 2006. The letter read as follows:

Mr Shujaat Husain
(My address)

8th February 2006

Dear Sir,

Re: Yourself-v-The Chief Constable of Kent
Case Number: 1100018/2005

Given the decision of the Ashford Employment Tribunals dated 31st October 2005, it is felt appropriate that a written apology should be offered to you for the actions of Kent Police, namely:

1. The rejection of your April 2000 application for the post of Intelligence Analyst.

2. The conception and depiction of you as a criminal who should be arrested and criminally prosecuted.

3. The investigations into your background undertaken by DC Clive Russell were totally perfunctory.

4. The collusion of the Force with Avon & Somerset Police, which resulted in the contamination of your application for employment with that Force.

The Tribunal has found that these actions were as a result of direct race discrimination and for this I am genuinely sorry.

Yours faithfully

Michael Fuller
Chief Constable

I felt elated at having been held in some esteem by the tribunal but was not very impressed by the tone of the apology tendered by the Chief Constable. It seemed to have been written under duress and only when the man had been literally ordered to do so by the court. His words seemed to lack genuine feeling, and he had just taken the exact text of the judgement and used it in his letter. It was as though he seemed to want to get rid of the entire matter once and for all by writing the letter. I do not know what he did after sending me the apology or what improvements (if any at all) were brought about in the Kent Police and their recruitment practices. Certainly, I was not contacted by anyone in the force in any way thereafter. The minimum I would have expected the Chief Constable to do was to charge the principal offenders (Richard Anderson and Clive Russell) and possibly dismiss them from the force altogether as a matter of procedure or a form of exemplary punishment. I don't believe any action was taken against the offenders. I received no further news on the fate of these policemen after that.

Seven

Conclusions and Recommendations

I for one would never have believed that the British policemen would stoop so low as to victimise a minority member based solely on his race, religion, or skin colour. Despite forcefully denying during more than five years of litigation that they had discriminated against me in any way, the accused parties were found to have discriminated in full measure. They tried in desperation to blame each other for the actions. The Kent Police claimed that, as the arrest was carried out by the other police force, it was not to be blamed. The other two, on the other hand, wove all sorts of tales to put the blame entirely on Kent Police, as Kent supposedly had initiated the rubbish. It was, nonetheless, a most serious case of institutionalised race discrimination, which the British police forces seem to be full of, despite their rebuttals and their claims that British society is a melting pot and discrimination is on the wane. It certainly is not. In my case, this was indicated to by the award of exemplary and aggravated damages. Race discrimination in Western societies (indeed, all over the world) and in the police forces is mostly subconscious (rather than conscious); in other words, the offenders, without consciously stating or expressing their racial prejudices, automatically presume minority members (those of colour or of ethnic or religious backgrounds that are different from their own) to be in some way less or different and then begin proving this to themselves and others in the most perverse of ways.

Most (if not all) of the allegations levelled by these subconscious racists are baseless or, at best, gross exaggerations, often with a malicious twist. This is precisely what happened when the police forces decided that my assertions on the job applications and CV must be false and set about trying to prove this to be the case, never considering making similar assumptions about other white "majority" applicants. Little is said or done consciously to show discrimination, but the behaviour is so offensive, malicious, and perverse (at times even through body language) that it can only be classified as discriminatory. In this matter, the falsity of each one of the allegations the police forces levelled against me proved the claim of discrimination conclusively. The aggravating factor was that the criminal case against me was built up clandestinely for well over a year by the collusion of these three police forces, at no time giving me any chance of an explanation or rebuttal. To make matters worse, this was the behaviour of detective constables, detective sergeants, and superintendents all around, who boasted of over twenty years of policing experience each! It is, of course, another matter that none of these highly trained and highly paid policemen ever took any step whatsoever during all this time to collect a shred of evidence to back up or rebut literally *any* of their nonsensical allegations.

If they had bothered to do their jobs properly, they would have been long satisfied. But this is precisely the point: they forget all reason and rationality and training when they see a member of a minority before them. It is worth stating here that almost all the policemen involved in this matter seemed to blab like parrots their own versions of the so-called "equal opportunities employment law" that they had been trained in. It is, of course, another matter that they had blown to smithereens this very same concept when it came to actual hiring practices, where they not only failed to give me an equal opportunity to be hired but, instead, harassed me because I'd innocently dared to ask for such an opportunity. I found it truly sickening.

The term "institutional racism" was coined by Stokely Carmichael, the Black Power activist, in the late 1960s. It was further expounded by William Macpherson, who made an in-depth enquiry in 1998 into the activities of another British police force regarding the murder of Stephen Lawrence, a Black youngster from Eltham, South London, by five white youths in April 1993. Macpherson described institutional racism as "the collective failure of an organisation to provide an appropriate and professional service to people because of their colour, culture or ethnic origin." When racism becomes integral to institutions, it becomes the accepted norm within the institution, making it difficult to highlight and rectify. When it is built into the institution, it appears as the collective action of the entire institution."

In the words of Mr A. Sivanandan, director of the Institute of Race Relations, "Institutional racism is that which, covertly or overtly, resides in the policies, procedures, operations and culture of public or private institutions – reinforcing individual prejudices and being reinforced by them in turn." It is especially prevalent among British police forces, as can be seen by the awards of the largest sums made by tribunals against precisely these organisations. These police forces seem only too eager to, and gleeful about, targeting minorities, especially Muslim and black youngsters. Despite the forces' denials and rebuttals and claims of so-called "training courses" fighting racism, which British policemen seem only too happy to talk about, the sceptre of institutional racism is the actual scenario prevailing in almost all of Britain's police forces today. It cannot (and should not) be mitigated by denial of facts and by the oft repeated statement that "it is more of an exception rather than the norm."

Institutional racism is compounded by the sceptre of Islamic fundamentalism and so-called Islamic terrorism that has become the talk of the dinner tables in British homes today. The spread of bigotry targeted at the Muslim community within the general public is, of course, linked strongly to the prolific lies and deceptions of British politicians and leaders, leading to the demonising of Muslims in Britain and of Muslim countries in general. Would it not be correct to state that these three British police forces (involving at least twelve white, Anglican Britons of all ranks) along with their legal advisors collectively pitting themselves against me for nearly six years was just another prime example of institutional racism? If this was not racism institutionalised, then what was it? And then what precisely *is* institutional racism if this was not such, I am compelled to ask?

Many claim that it is actually the uniform and the so-called naked powers of arrest, apprehension, and interrogation given to the police (all power for the police and no power for the other) that make police officers abuse these powers so easily and wilfully in their day-to-day duties. In actual fact, policemen exhibit arrogance and a form of profound stupidity in this abuse. Whereas, in less privileged countries, the police are often rightly accused of other evils (such as the use of third-degree methods of interrogation, the use of torture, and rampant corruption, to name just a few) the British police force is infamous for its singularly racist behaviour. The racism could be in-house, against minority members of its own community or, more commonly, projected outwards, against minorities from among the public. In efforts to lessen institutional racism, I would recommend that at least some of the powers should be given to private organisations, which would run on a profit motive, be staffed mostly by minorities, and have a vetted interest in obeying anti-discrimination laws.

If this level of racism in the British police is to be seriously tackled, it has to be accepted as rampant and, as an initial measure, any uniformed police officer found guilty of even a minor offence should be charge sheeted and given the maximum punishment of dismissal from service (without benefits). A major offence (such as an incidence of conscious discrimination or stereotyping or unjustified physical abuse of a minority) should entail a further penalty of being charged with a racially aggravated offence with criminal sanction. Further, in all incidents, the accused officer should be replaced in his police force with a member of the same race or community he has mistreated. Less, different or derogatory treatment of a minority by a member of the force should, in and of itself, be taken to be sufficient and necessary evidence of discrimination; no conscious remark or stereotyping should be required. This is rectification by penalty and not just by supposed "retraining" or vetting of the accused, as frequently happens. The senior most commanders of police forces should hold as their motto zero tolerance against racism, which includes exemplary punishment for the guilty members as a means of maximal deterrence.

Sadly, such a motto may be present only *de jure* but certainly not *de facto* in its present state.

If one were to accept that the British police forces are, indeed, fundamentally racist, as I believe them to be, what may be said of the tribunals and the judiciary? I have had a lot of exposure to British tribunals, and I may state with confidence that I have very seldom seen or experienced any so-called white tribunal ruling in favour of a minority claimant. They all seem to strike out the claim on virtually no evidence or on the flimsiest of evidence, frequently just taking the respondent on his or her word, despite all evidence to the contrary. This is what I experienced in Cardiff (more than once) and then in Bristol. What also adds weight to this scenario is that the only finding in my favour came when the Chairperson was a Black lady, who carried out detailed cross-examinations of the witnesses, which the other chairmen (as well as the lay members) singularly failed to do.

The Ashford Judgement was in stark contrast to the other two, which were based almost on the same evidence. It fully gave the justice that should have been given all along. I was upset at the teams of barristers and solicitors all around for not making their clients come to a settlement but, perhaps, even more angered by the virtually openly biased judgements of these tribunals. They did not seem to be worth the paper they were written on. To give an example, the Judgement of the Bristol Tribunal described the enquiry reports prepared by the South Wales Police as "profoundly flawed" but then actually praised the policemen who had written them and fully exonerated them! No cross-examination of the accused was done by the Chairman or his colleagues at any time, when a full day could easily have been spent in breaking each one of these characters down. In the Cardiff matter, I filed a complaint with the President of the Tribunals against the Chairman. I never received a reply. It hardly mattered, as it only made me come to the poignant conclusion that the tribunals themselves were not very far behind the police in their own version of discrimination against minorities.

One has to accept that these tribunals are comprised of predominantly upper middle class, white Christians who, even with their level of education and examination, are probably not trained or accustomed to seeing anyone of their own kind as guilty of anything, least of all discrimination in employment. Certainly, they don't seem to like that one or more of their own kind stands accused of anything at all. This is indicated to by their body language and even post-judgement comments. Here again, discrimination is subconscious and difficult to pinpoint, but this does not imply that it doesn't exist. One of the chairmen involved in this matter is reported to have stated (some time before I filed the appeal) that I had collected an amount in excess of £75,000 from the schools as a result of filing claims against them! It was a most bizarre and, of course, preposterous statement. I felt strongly about the inappropriateness of his allegations and seriously considered initiating proceedings for defamation. I feel that the Bar Council should make the process of qualification, training, and vetting of its qualifiers (and future Chairmen) more thorough and stringent.

Moreover, Tribunals should now be composed of increasing numbers of minorities, particularly Chairmen who hail from Asian and Black communities. As a trial and in attempts to prove facts, I would also recommend that the same case (or scenario) should be tried independently by a "white" tribunal and a "minority" tribunal (a tribunal comprised entirely of minority members) and then to see if the tribunals reached the same judgement and findings. If the results are markedly different, this essentially would mean that the British judiciary has failed the acid test and needs in-depth reformation and self-examination. Further, efforts should be made to ensure that a minority claim (or a claim involving a minority) should be handled by a minority chairman rather than a white one. Critics of this line of thought are quick to point out that this would, in fact, be discrimination, as the judiciary does not look up the racial profiling of its members. But this simply is not a good enough argument and cannot be used if the interests of justice are to be kept supreme.

Further, due mainly to the current national and international situation and the increasing discrimination by police and the public alike against Muslims, per se, it is also my recommendation that the Race Relations Act of 1975 should be amended to include religion (along with race, colour, sex, age, nationality, and ethnic origins) as a basis of discrimination in employment. Currently, there is no basis on which discrimination on grounds of religion is to be claimed, the only redressal being to include religious affiliation as part of race. But the incidence of discrimination on the grounds of religion is now commonplace enough to justify its inclusion in and of itself as a basis. Certainly, this will raise awareness to the increasing prevalence of discrimination in British society and may well cause it to abate.

It is very easy to deny or downplay the existence of something like institutional racism, but it is never a good idea to sweep the dirt under the rug rather than to expose it and clean it out. It is never easy in most claims based on what is referred to as subconscious discrimination to pinpoint with accuracy the precise basis of the differing treatment or behaviour, so it is best to give tribunals the discretion to determine this during the hearings.

It is also to be understood and I think accepted by all that considerable authority lies with the initial court hearing the evidence including, crucially, the cross-examination of the witnesses. A decision made by a tribunal in the case of a discrimination claim is appealable to the higher court only on a point of law and not on a point of fact. In other words, it should be based on legal errors alone or a wrong application of the law. Considerable discretion is given to the Chairmen and lay members to take any evidence as relevant in their findings. Virtually no appeals are admitted on factual evidence alone. Only a judgement that is blatantly wrong on the evidence is taken as being appealable in and of itself. This lays considerable authority with the lower court with regard to the merits of the case. In this case the absolute integrity, competence, and honesty of the tribunals are of the utmost importance. Not in every matter adjudicated do tribunals exhibit this integrity and honesty to the highest level or even to the level required. As such, I feel that the higher court should interfere and set the record straight and not leave all to the mercy of the lower court. Leaving it as such will (and frequently does) lead to a miscarriage of justice. In other words, appeals should be admissible to the higher court even on the absence of a thorough (or proper) examination of the evidence or of the witnesses by the Tribunal, or even in the absence of such evidence at all.

I recall that, during a hearing, a Chairman in the Watford Tribunals directly accused me, saying that he had "found" that I had lied to him and his Tribunal at the conclusion of the hearing. His manner of speech was bombastic and crude. When queried as to what his so-called "findings" were based on (such as independent witness evidence, recordings of conversations, and the like) he was unable to give any answer. It was a serious allegation by a member of the judiciary and absolutely baseless. It turned out that, just on a balance of probabilities, he had taken the word of the respondents against mine. It was, of course, another matter that the two respondents (both white) were in actual fact lying in unison and with premeditation. But this Chairman and his lay members were pathetically unable to see this! I was at a loss but was told that this was not appealable, as it was based on facts and did not amount to an error of law. I filed a complaint, but it was not satisfactorily replied to.

Further tribunals and, in particular, Chairmen (even part-time) should be vetted and graded on their abilities and competence and should not be given live hearings until they come out well on the evaluations and score high on the gradations. The Bar Council could play a useful role in this context. Justice should be even-handed and imparted without regard to race or skin colour of any party. However, this is easier said than done. Until that is accomplished, the future of the "minorities" in Britain, who form nearly 10 per cent of the national population and nearly a third of the population of greater London, will be pretty much in limbo.

RESERVED JUDGEMENT

EMPLOYMENT TRIBUNALS

BETWEEN

<u>Claimant</u>

Mr Shujaat Husain

<u>Respondent</u>

The Chief Constable

of Kent County Constabulary

JUDGMENT OF THE EMPLOYMENT TRIBUNAL

HELD AT: Ashford, Kent

ON: 25, 26, 27 and 28 July and
(in chambers on 28 and 29 July)
2005

CHAIRMAN: Ms C Hyde

MEMBERS: Mr. M J Blackwell
Mr T J Gallagher

Appearances:

For Claimant: In person
For Respondent: Miss S Garner of Counsel

JUDGMENT

The unanimous judgment of the Tribunal is that

1. The Claimant's complaint of direct race discrimination in respect of
   the rejection of his April 2000 application for a job is well founded

(part of paragraph 10(a) of the Particulars of Discrimination dated 31 March 2004);

2.   The Claimant's complaint of direct race discrimination by the Respondent in respect of the conception and depiction of the Claimant as a criminal who should be arrested and criminally prosecuted is well founded (paragraph 10(b) of the Particulars of Discrimination dated 31 March 2004);

3.   The Claimant's complaint of direct race discrimination in that the investigations into his background made by the Respondent were totally perfunctory is well founded (part of paragraph 109d) of the Particulars of Discrimination dated 31 March 2004);

4.   The Claimant's complaint of direct race discrimination in that the Respondent through Mr R Anderson and Mr Russell colluded with the Avon & Somerset Police resulting in the contamination of the Claimant's application for employment is well founded (part of paragraph 10(g) of the Particulars of Discrimination dated 31 March 2004);

5.   The Tribunal will reconvene on a date to be notified to the parties in order to determine remedy in respect of the above matters;

6.   The Claimant's complaint of race discrimination in respect of his application for a job with the Respondent in 1999 is not well founded and is therefore dismissed (part of paragraph 10(a) of the Particulars of Discrimination dated 31 March 2004);

7.   The Claimant's complaint of race discrimination in respect of his application for a job with the South Wales Police in about May 2000 is not well founded and is therefore dismissed (part

of paragraph 10(a) of the Particulars of Discrimination dated 31 March 2004);

8. The Claimant's complaint of race discrimination in respect of his application for a job with the Avon and Somerset Police in 2000 is not well founded and is therefore dismissed (part of paragraph 10(a) of the Particulars of Discrimination dated 31 March 2004;

9. The Claimant's complaint about the falsity of the allegations of criminal deception being an act of race discrimination is not well founded and is dismissed, being a matter already determined by the Bristol Employment Tribunal (paragraph 10(c) of the Particulars of Discrimination dated 31 March 2004);

10. The complaints of the Claimant about his arrest and incarceration by the Avon and Somerset Police in paragraphs 10(e) and (f) of the Particulars of Discrimination dated 31 March 2004 are not well founded and are therefore dismissed, being matters already determined by the Bristol Employment Tribunal; and

11. The Claimant's complaint that the Respondent aided and abetted the South Wales Police and the Avon and Somerset Police to discriminate against him on racial grounds is not well founded and is therefore dismissed.

REASONS

1. By an Originating Application which was presented in the Cardiff Employment Tribunal on 25 January 2001, Mr Husain brought a claim of race discrimination. The claim was subsequently amended and by the date of the hearing in the Ashford Tribunal, the Tribunal proceeded on the basis of the document which was presented on 30 March 2004, with the accompanying particulars

of aiding and abetting presented on 17 March 2004. The Tribunal proceeded on the basis of the re-amended Notice of Appearance which was undated and was found at pages 27-31 of the hearing bundle. The Claimant also submitted a questionnaire under the Race Relations Act 1976 on 25 January 2001. Correspondence from the Respondent to the Cardiff Law Centre which was chasing a response indicates that the answers were "being worked on" up to 5 April 2001. The Respondent finally replied under cover of a letter dated 12 November 2004.

2. The Tribunal heard evidence from the Claimant in person. His witness statement comprised of his evidence in chief was [C3]. During his case, the Claimant relied on the witness statement of Mr Keith Jackson, Principal Criminal Intelligence Analyst in the Force Intelligence Group of Avon and Somerset Constabulary [C4]. The witness statement had been adduced by the Avon and Somerset Police in the proceedings brought about by the Claimant in the Bristol Employment Tribunal.

3. In addition, the Tribunal considered a skeleton argument at the outset of the Claimant's case [C1], an additional bundle of documents prepared by the Claimant [C2] and a schedule of loss [C5]. Finally, the Claimant's closing submission was marked [C6].

4. The main documents which comprised an agreed bundle were in two lever arch files continuously numbered and marked [R1]. The Tribunal was largely concerned with the first of these files constituting some 200 pages. The Tribunal also considered the witness statement of Mr Kenneth Colbeck, Detective Constable serving in the Avon and Somerset Constabulary, which had also been provided for the Bristol Employment Tribunal case [R3]. A copy of the judgment and reasons of the Bristol Employment

Tribunal which were sent to the parties on 6 July 2005 [R5] was also considered. The decision of the Tribunal was that the Claimant's complaint of race discrimination against the Avon and Somerset Police was dismissed. The Tribunal further considered the witness statement of Mr Geoffrey Anderson, who at the time of the matters complained against of in this case held the rank of Chief Inspector posted to the Operational Crime Group at headquarters CID in the Avon and Somerset Police. His witness statement was presented to the Bristol Employment Tribunal [R7]. Similarly, the Tribunal considered the witness statement of Mr David Jones, a member of the Financial Investigation Unit at Avon and Somerset Constabulary, who was previously a Sergeant in the Police Force. His witness statement had similarly been prepared for the Bristol Employment Tribunal case [R8]. Further witness statements of Chief Superintendent 273 J B Adsley of SWP adduced in the Cardiff Employment Tribunal proceedings were in the bundles prepared for the Tribunal.

5. At the commencement of the hearing, Miss Garner presented a chronology [R6] and an opening submission [R10], both of which the Tribunal read at the outset. Finally, Miss Garner presented a written closing submission at the end of the case [R12].

6. On behalf of the Respondent, the Tribunal heard evidence from Detective Constable Clive Russell of the Kent Police, currently Intelligence Analyst Trainer, but previously a member of the Special Branch. The second witness for the Respondent was Detective Constable Charis White of the South Wales Police based at the time that is relevant to these proceedings in the Special Branch at Cardiff.

7. The next witness was Mr Gregory Kirk, employed by the Kent Police as a legal services lawyer within the Legal Services Department.

His witness statement was labelled [R5]. The evidence was adduced at the request of the Tribunal in order to explain issues relating to disclosure of documents by the Respondent. The Tribunal queried the absence of any comparative documentation in respect of the 1999 recruitment, such as the details of the successful candidate, which should in the normal course have been retained on their personnel file. This information ought to have been available when the claim was presented in January 2001.

8. Finally, the Tribunal heard evidence from Mr Richard Anderson, currently employed by Kent Police as the Head of Intelligence Analyst Training. Between October 1994 and May 2000, he was employed as the Principal Analyst working at Force headquarters in Maidstone. His witness statement was marked [R11].

Relevant Background/Issues

9. Mr Husain complained that he was discriminated against when he made his job applications to the Respondent in August 1999 and April 2000, in that his applications were refused for reasons connected to his race. Although on its face, Mr Husain's claim to the Tribunal appears straightforward, the reality was somewhat more complex. Mr Husain was arrested by the Avon and Somerset Constabulary ("A & S") after he had applied to them for a job in about August 2000. On 10 January 2001, he was detained and questioned by the A & S Police, his local Police Force at the time, in respect of attempting to obtain a pecuniary advantage (the job he applied for) by deception. The deceptions alleged related to details he had provided in support of his job applications to A & S and other Forces, including his academic qualifications and professional experience and training. Although somewhat shocked and disorientated by the arrest, Mr Husain fully cooperated with the Police. After being detained for some hours he was released in

order for enquiries to be made to establish the truth or otherwise of the information he had provided. Following the interview and a period of detention, the Claimant was accompanied by police officers to his home address, which was searched in order to obtain information which the Claimant indicated would exculpate him completely.

10. In a report dated 19 January 2001 from D/C Colbeck of the A&S Constabulary relating to the Claimant, Mr Colbeck described how the results of their telephone enquiries and the viewing of documents produced by the Claimant when his property was searched satisfied him about the truth of the matters set out in his application. He recommended the following courses of action:

    (1) That a letter be sent to Mr Husain and his legal representative releasing him from his bail commitment;
    (2) That a copy of Mr Colbeck's report be forwarded to Kent County Constabulary and South Wales Constabulary in order that their records be updated; and
    (3) That consideration be given to an All Forces Bulletin being broadcast regarding Mr Husain.

11. The Tribunal was unable to verify whether the second and third courses of action recommended by Mr Colbeck had actually been carried through. However, it appeared obvious to the Tribunal that Mr Colbeck appreciated the damage that had been done and could continue to be done to Mr Husain's reputation if the corrections were not as widely circulated as the erroneous report and accounts had been. Sadly however, even this report contained a gratuitous and unsubstantiated comment about Mr Husain having been given a different certificate from the rest of the officers on completion of a course with the Northumbria Police. The Tribunal had the

benefit of seeing Mr Husain's certificate. It was not in the terms described by Mr Colbeck or his source in Northumbria Police.

12. It was as a result of his arrest and questioning in January 2001 that Mr Husain learned that his job applications had generated suspicion across more than one Force. The applications for positions with A & S Police, South Wales Police ("SWP") and Kent County Constabulary were cited in the interview under caution as being the matters that the charges were based on.

13. On 25 January 2001 Mr Husain presented a claim against the Respondent and the Chief Constable of South Wales Police and the Chief Constable of Avon and Somerset Police in the Cardiff Employment Tribunal. The application consisted of three claims of direct race discrimination arising from the Claimant's applications for jobs with each of the three Forces, which were turned down.

14. In due course, after a considerable number of Employment Tribunal interlocutory hearings, the claims against each Respondent were dealt with separately in their local Tribunals. The claim against SWP was heard by the Cardiff Employment Tribunal and dismissed on the ground that it was not brought within three months of the date of the act complained of. The Claimant knew he had not been short listed for the SWP job in about June 2000. This decision was appealed against twice by the Claimant and finally confirmed by the Court of Appeal on 9 June 2005.

15. The A&S claim was heard by the Bristol Employment Tribunal between 20 and 22 June 2005. Judgment was sent to the parties on 5 July 2005. The decision of the Bristol Employment Tribunal was that A&S had not unlawfully discriminated against the Claimant in their treatment of him on racial grounds and the claim was therefore not well-founded.

16. Along with the claim of direct discrimination against the Respondent, in March 2004 the Claimant amended his claim to include an allegation the Respondent has perpetrated further acts of discrimination under section 33(1) of the Race Relations Act 1976 ("the 1976 Act") by knowingly aiding SWP and A&S in their unlawful acts of discrimination against him.

17. The issue then arose in this Tribunal as to how far, if at all, the Tribunal could encroach on issues already determined in some respects by the Cardiff and Bristol Employment Tribunals. The Tribunal had to determine how it should deal with the parts of the Claimant's claim which related to the Respondent (Kent) having aided and abetted A&S in unlawfully discriminating against him.

18. The Respondent submitted that the Tribunal in the current case was bound by the judgment of the Bristol Employment Tribunal insofar as it concluded that A&S had not unlawfully discriminated against the Claimant. This submission was based on two arguments. The first was that Kent denied providing assistance knowingly within the meaning of section 33(1) of the 1976 Act in any event. However, even if the Tribunal did not agree with that primary submission, the Respondent submitted that Kent could not have committed an unlawful act of discrimination by knowingly aiding A&S to do an act which was not, as determined by the Bristol Employment Tribunal, unlawful within the meaning of the 1976 Act.

19. Further, Miss Garner submitted that the findings of fact on the part of the Bristol Employment Tribunal were persuasive rather than binding on the Tribunal.

20. In relation to the SWP aiding and abetting claim, there had not been a hearing on the merits of the case against the SWP. Therefore, no

Tribunal had adjudicated on the question of whether SWP had discriminated unlawfully against the Claimant. The proceedings had been dismissed on the basis that the Claimant had brought his claim out of time. Kent Acknowledged that there were no known cases under section 33(1) in which the claims brought against the main perpetrator and the party accused of knowingly aiding the perpetrator had been dealt with at different times. Thus, although the Respondent called a witness from South Wales Police, D/C/ White, Couth Wales Police was not represented at the hearing of the current claim. The situation raised certain questions in relation to the interplay between section 33 and the burden of proof provision under section 54A. Kent's position was that in the circumstances of this case, the primary act of discrimination had to be proved, i.e. unlawful discrimination on the part of SWP, in its entirety by the Claimant, in order to comply with the principles in *Igen Ltd –v—Wong* **[2005] IRLR 258.**

21. Kent further submitted that the Claimant also had to prove that aid was provided knowingly to SWP by Kent in the committing of the alleged unlawful act of discrimination. It was only if the Claimant succeeded in establishing those matters that the burden of proof switched to the Respondent to prove on the balance of probabilities that its actions were for a reason unconnected with race.

22. The actions of SWP which the Claimant complained about and alleged to be racially discriminatory were in failing to progress his application for a similar job.

Facts Found

23. The Claimant is of Pakistani national origin and arrived in the United Kingdom in April 1999. He was formerly a high-ranking career police officer with the Pakistan Police and had an impressive

academic background and considerable experience in policing including intelligence functions.

24. The Claimant applied for employment with various police forces in the United Kingdom for which he clearly had suitable experience and qualifications. Aside from the academic qualification and other experience set out elsewhere in these Reasons, Mr Husain was proficient in a number of European and Asian languages, including French and to a lesser degree, Arabic. His racial and ethnic origin is obviously inferred from the information provided in the job application forms and resumes submitted by him.

25. In about August 1999, shortly after his arrival in the country, the Claimant applied for the post of Intelligence Analyst with the Kent County Constabulary, based at Dover ("the 1999 application"). Mr Husain was short listed and interviewed for the position. Following the psychometric tests and interview, the Claimant was informed that he was unsuccessful. He was sent a letter by Ms Jean Craft (Personnel) informing him of the outcome of his application, in which she referred to him having come 'a close second'. The Tribunal had to decide whether to accept that this comment had been made in the letter following the 1999 application. It was relevant to the case put forward by the Respondent that the Claimant had performed poorly at the interview in September 1999 and that was why Mr Anderson, who also was present at the interview along with Ms Craft and DCI Holmes in 1999, had decided when the Claimant applied some seven months later in April 2000 for a similar post of Intelligence Analyst, not to put Mr Husain's application forward to interview. Neither Ms Craft nor Mr Holmes gave evidence to the Tribunal.

26. Mr Husain also repeated this comment during his interview under caution by A & S Police in January 2001.

27. The Tribunal could not assess the truth of the statement by reference to contemporaneous documents. It was a regrettable fact in this case that apart from the Claimant's own application forms in relation to the 1999 application, along with the interview marking sheets for his interview, and the page which contained the Claimant's name on the log setting out details of when people applied for jobs and whether they were given interviews, there were no other documents relating to the 1999 application process. The documents available to the Tribunal were those in existence at the time of the Claimant's application for an extension of time at the Ashford Tribunal. The Respondent had no written policy relating to the retention and disposal of documents arising from a recruitment process in 1999 or 2000. It was accepted practice at the time for such papers to be held for between 6 months and if possible up to two years following the appointment to the vacant post. In practice, the period of retention of documents was dependent on storage capacity in each |Policing Area, which were varied across the County. Mr Husain's 1999 recruitment papers, such as they were, were probably retained when they were provided in April 2000 to DC Russell as part of the enquiries. Mr Kirk's evidence to the Tribunal that the Respondent had recently updated as part of a Force wide review, its policies on the retention of such documents, was accepted. Thus a 2 year retention policy now applied to such papers.

28. The Respondent did not appear to have endeavoured, before the Tribunal requested this during the hearing, to track down the details of the successful candidate in the 1999 recruitment process.

29. Given the circumstance outlined above, it was not surprising that the Tribunal could not be provided with the necessary comparator evidence in 2005.

30. The Tribunal considered that the absence of the contemporaneous documents relating to the 1999 recruitment was unsatisfactory. It was thus impossible to know, by comparison with the successful candidate for example, or with other candidates who were interviewed, whether the marks given to the Claimant on the interview marking sheets indicted that it was likely he had come 'a close second' and therefore had not had a poor interview. The relevant witness on behalf of the Respondent, Mr R. Anderson, indicated that he had conducted many hundreds of interview but that he particularly remembered the interview of the Claimant.

31. Although Mr Husain did not produce the letter from the Respondent containing the reference to his having come a close second in respect of his 1999 application, he included that comment on the front page of his April 2000 application form where he was asked whether he had applied for any other post in the Constabulary in the preceding two years and for details of the title and approximate date of the most recent application and whether he had been interviewed. He also referred to that comment when he set out, as he was required to in his own handwriting, what were the reasons for the application. Towards the end of his explanation, he stated as follows:

> *"I was very disappointed in not*
> *having been selected last time, but*
> *was informed that I was very close*
> *to it. I have gained much in the*
> *interim period . . ."*

32. The Tribunal considered that this was the sort of matter that the Claimant was more likely to have recollected than Mr Anderson, because it was comment which was of considerably more

significance to the Claimant at the time it was made. The Tribunal also found Claimant's evidence generally to be extremely reliable and truthful. The circumstances in which Mr Husain had related the comment were also relevant. He had set them out in the job application to the same potential employer, who he believed had made the comment in the first place. The application was also written within a year after the rejection letter was written. Mr Anderson did not profess to have seen the rejection letter which was written by Ms Craft, although the report by Ms White in May 2000 referred to Mr Russell having told her that Mr Husain had performed poorly in his interview in August 1999. The Tribunal accepted that this report came from Mr Anderson.

33. Mr R Anderson did not provide any distinguishing detail to the Tribunal about the Claimant's interview or the results of the psychometric testing, beyond the information recorded on the interview record sheet. In his evidence in chief he acknowledged that there was no practice within the Respondent at the time of not re-interviewing previously unsuccessful candidates in recent recruitment exercises. Mr R Anderson's background had been to develop procedures relating to, among other things, recruitment, for Intelligence Analysts.

34. He described noting during the paper sift in 2000 that Mr Husain's application as a whole was "remarkable". It was rare to get applications from foreign nationals, let alone such a candidate with a police intelligence background. He wanted to ensure that his recollection of the candidate who had previously applied in 1999 was correct therefore he asked for the 1999 papers. Mr Anderson pointed that Tribunal to what he perceived to be the following 'material differences' between the two applications:

(i) Different A levels stated on each form;

(ii) a failure to <u>highlight</u> (emphasis added) on his initial application that his best qualification was in fact a double honours degree; and

(iii) a reference in his application to "being very close" to being selected on his first application.

35. There were thus considerations which weighed on both sides. In all the circumstances however, on the balance of probabilities, the Tribunal accepted that truthfulness and accuracy of this comment made by Mr Husain.

36. In other respects the Tribunal was unable to rely on Mr Anderson's evidence about matters which occurred in about 2000 concerning Mr Husain. The following is one example. In their respective witness statements Mr Russell and Mr R Anderson both set out the circumstances in which Mr Russell came to investigate Mr Husain's application and the outcome and conclusion of the investigation. Both referred to having a meeting with a senior officer, Superintendent Philpot, about what should be done with the investigation. Mr Anderson reported that the discussion took place after Mr Russell had conducted his 'initial enquiries' and that Mr Philpot had advised them not to pursue the matter. Mr Russell described speaking to Mr Philpot before conducting his 'initial enquiries' and that Mr Philpot had told him that Kent Police would not wish to prosecute the case but that he should make some initial enquiries. He did not in his witness statement or in his oral evidence describe meeting Mr Philpot again about the issue. Ms White's report dated 31 May 2000 refers to Mr Russell awaiting results of enquiries from Karachi and that he was considering criminal charges against Mr Husain.

37. It was apparent from the two application forms that the Claimant had taken steps in the period between the two applications to become more familiar with the job of an Intelligence Analyst. Thus there were more relevant points referred to in his later application. This signalled to the Tribunal that the Claimant was keen to improve his chances of being selected for such as post, and that it was by no means certain that Mr Husain's performance at interview in 2000 would not have been an improvement on his 1999 performance.

38. The erroneous conclusions as a result of what the Tribunal was driven to conclude were perfunctory enquiries about the US qualifications and the attendance on a course with Northumbria Police on the part of D/C Russell were contained in a report by D/C White of SW Police Special Branch dated 31 May 2000. This report was sent to D/I Cotterell of Bridgend Special Branch. The report also contained further erroneous findings by D/C White, for example about whether the Claimant had truly been given admission to a PhD programme in Criminology at the University of Wales, Cardiff. This information was gained as a result of speaking to "reliable contacts" at the University of Wales. In the event it was completely inaccurate. Mr Husain had been offered a place in three years (1995, 96 and 99) but had been unable to take it up on each occasion due to financial constraints.

39. The Tribunal also had to determine what were the areas of suspicion for Kent Police at the time. Judging by the areas that Mr Russell investigated it was the MIT degree and the Northumbria course. Later, during these proceedings other issues were raised, like a discrepancy between the A levels obtained (in the questionnaire replies). As Mr Husain stated in his applications that the A level qualifications were awarded by the University of Cambridge and

London Local Examinations Syndicates, the Tribunal struggled to see why no attempt was apparently made to verify this either in 2000 or subsequently. Equally Mr Husain could have been asked to produce his certificates. In fact he was awarded all the qualifications mentioned on his applications. He achieved 5 A levels in high grades in 1974. He listed the Mathematics, Physics, Economics and English in his first application in his first application and omitted the English but listed Pure Maths instead in his second. Either list of A levels would have amply met the criteria for the posts applied for.

40. It was clear to the Tribunal that Mr Husain had achieved academic success well above that which would normally be expected of a candidate for such as post. In addition the A level qualifications should have been relevant background but less significant than Mr Husain's degree and subsequent work experience in the succeeding 25 years.

41. The Tribunal was particularly troubled by the enquiries made by Mr Russell in relation to the Northumbria Police course and of the Massachusetts Institute of Technology ("MIT").

42. Mr Russell did not give his evidence in a very convincing or compelling manner. The Tribunal took into account that he was giving evidence about matters which were now some five years old. There was also a conflict of evidence between Mr Russell and Ms White. She had recorded the results of her enquiries at the time in the report to Mr Cotterell. She distinguished in that report between matters that she had enquired into herself and matters that she had discovered from Mr Russell. Given that it was relatively contemporaneous (dated 31 May 2000), and consistent with other evidence, the Tribunal considered it to be a reliable record.

43. By the time for the hearing, there was no dispute that Mr Husain had attended a Traffic Police/Engineers course in 1994 run by the Northumbria Police in Newcastle upon Tyne – not a surveillance course. This information was contained in a CV, which accompanied his application in 1999 and was also subsequently set out in the application form in the Claimant's handwriting in his 2000 application. When Mr Russell spoke to Ms White, he reported that the Claimant had actually attended a surveillance course for police officers from overseas forces and that "it had been swiftly terminated as the students were so bad – they wore their covert radio equipment outside their clothing among other facts."

44. This account was very far from the truth and demeaning of the participants. Ms White's report confirms that it was known in May 2000 that the participants on the course were from overseas forces. In fact, as was confirmed by Mr Husain in his evidence, there were eight Police officers on the course, all of whom were Pakistani. It was a course funded by the World Bank, and was linked to the establishment of a Traffic Training Institute in Karachi. The course lasted for six weeks. It was not terminated prematurely. All participants including Mr Husain were awarded certificates, and on his return to Pakistan, Mr Husain took up a posting as Principal of the new Institute, for which the course had helped equip him.

45. Another concerning aspect of Mr Russell's involvement in this enquiry was that he sought in his witness statement to distance himself from the enquiry of Northumbria Police and its recorded results. During his evidence he initially denied having contacted the Northumbria Police but reported that he was aware that there were anecdotes going around to the effect stated in Ms White's report. In due course he accepted that he may have been the source of the information in Ms White's report albeit that he only

conveyed the 'anecdote' to her. When Ms White gave evidence, she was clear that she had obtained her information from Mr Russell and that as recorded in her reasonably contemporaneous report of 31 May 2000, Northumbria Police informed her that Mr Russell had made an enquiry about Mr Husain and attending the course. That was why she had not pursued her own independent enquiry of that Force. The Tribunal was not made aware of anyone else in Kent Police who had been asked to enquire into Mr Husain's background.

46. The Tribunal was therefore satisfied on the balance of probabilities that the enquiries had been made by Mr Russell of the Northumbria Police and that his vagueness around his involvement and the distorted report that was then conveyed to Ms White were indicative of his approach to the task.

47. Mr Russell's evidence about his enquiry about Mr Husain's qualifications in the United States also caused the Tribunal some concern. The true position, as stated by Mr Husain in his applications was that he had obtained a double Honours degree in Economics and Electrical Engineering from MIT at the end of a period of study form 1975 to 1982. He was awarded a full scholarship by MIT for the course of study. In his witness statement, Mr Russell reported that he had made a telephone enquiry to MIT and that they had checked their database and advised him that the only 'Husain' they were aware of was one of their cleaners and they suggested that he made further enquiries of another source. If this were an accurate account of what happened, the Tribunal considers it likely, as Mr Russell accepted in cross-examination, that he had enquired of someone who kept records relating to staff as opposed to the student body. The Tribunal also considered it surprising that if this were the case, Mr Russell had not conveyed to all the officers to whom he subsequently spoke about his enquiries in the context of

possible criminal charges, that they had been so perfunctory and that he had been invited to make some further enquiries in order to confirm the position about whether Mr Husain had been a member of the student body.

48. Mr Russell maintained in his oral evidence that his enquiries had only been preliminary or initial and were not intended to be relied upon. There was no hint in the witness statements or oral evidence of any of the officers or staff members of other Forces to whom Mr Russell spoke that this was the case. The evidence of Ms White was quite clear that she had not been told by Mr Russell that his enquiries were only preliminary or initial, or that MIT had suggested that he should contact somebody else. On the contrary, as the report of Ms White records, the Tribunal considered that the other officers would have been entitled to believe that there was a reasonable basis for Mr Russell's enquiries, given the he informed them that he was considering the possibility of criminal charges against Mr Husain as of May 2000. This view was consistent with the Reasons of the Bristol Tribunal which heard evidence forma the A & S staff. That Tribunal in its findings described that Mr Geoffrey Anderson believed that Mr Russell's inquiry had been 'robust' and the investigation and findings 'sound' and the Tribunal referred to Mr Russell's specialist experience in criminal intelligence gathering.

49. Mr Russell conducted his enquiry at the request of Mr Richard Anderson, who was at the time Principal Analyst. The Tribunal rejected Mr Anderson's account that he did not put Mr Husain through to the shortlisting stage in April 2000 because, "in line with the prevailing personnel practices", Mr Husain had been recently interviewed and had been unsuccessful. This phrase was first used in a short statement prepared by Mr Richard Anderson on 29 January 2002 and repeated in his witness statement in

this case. There was no such Personnel practice, prevailing or otherwise. It is likely that Mr Husain would otherwise have been shortlisted. Indeed the only page of the log recording the decisions at shortlisting stage which was available showed that out of six candidates recorded on that page, only one other was shortlisted, and that candidate's application had only demonstrated that she had met three of the five essential criteria for the job. In the circumstances the Tribunal did not find satisfactory the explanation for Mr Anderson withdrawing Mr Husain from the recruitment process in 2000.

50. The false information was confirmed by Mr Russell to the A&S staff when they contacted him again some considerable time later in January 2001. Mr Russell did not contradict the parts of the witness statements of the A&S officers which were put to him when he was giving his evidence in which he indicated that they contacted Mr Russell in order to verify the contents of Ms White's report. The Tribunal also considers that this tends to show that a copy of Ms White's report was sent to Mr Russell shortly after it was produced, as requested by her at the end of her report. She asks that the report and attachment be sent to Mr Russell at the Force Intelligence Bureau, Analyst's Department, Kent Police Headquarters.

51. Mr Russell was a former Special Branch officer.

52. An unsigned and undated manuscript note at the bottom of an email dated 9 May 2000 from Mr Davies of South Wales Special Branch to the National Security Services relating to investigation into the Claimant recorded, among other matters that Mr Russell stated that he had contacted MIT and that they had not heard of Mr Husain. Mr Russell accepted that he had spoken to South Wales Police and had conveyed the erroneous results of his enquiries

of MIT to them and SWP subsequently passed these on to the Security Services.

53. Further, Mr Russell spoke to Mr Jackson of A&S Police (Principal Criminal Intelligence Analyst) many times between about August and October 2000, and Mr Russell discussed with him the nature of any charge that A&S might proceed with. Mr Jackson was not a police officer and Mr Russell had a greater understanding and knowledge of criminal charges.

54. Mr Russell also accepted that he spoke to Mr Anderson of A&S Police some time in about September 2000.

55. He accepted that it appeared from the witness statements of Mr Jackson and Mr Anderson that they did not understand that he was placing any caveats around the information that he was passing on relating to Mr Husain. The Tribunal took into account that it did not hear directly from Mr Anderson or Mr Jackson or Mr Colbeck. However, insofar as the witness statements for the other proceedings appeared to be on similar lines to the evidence given by D/C White and as recorded by her in her contemporaneous report, the Tribunal considered that it was safe to assume, on the balance of probabilities that Mr Russell had spoken to the other officers in terms similar to those recorded by Ms White.

56. The Tribunal considered that Mr Russell was reckless about the effect on Mr Husain of his perfunctory enquiries, and of the effects of communicating the results to other Police Forces including Special Branch officers.

57. All the officers and staff referred to in these Reasons of the three Police Forces were White European. Within the two years prior to the date on which the Claimant's Race Relations Act questionnaire

was served, the Respondent employed two Intelligence Analysts from Minority Ethnic origins. As of September 2000, Kent Police employed 37 Police Officers, 31 civilian staff and 8 Special Constables of Minority Ethnic origins.

58. Mr Russell had worked alongside two Minority Ethnic officers (Black African) when working as a Liaison with Immigration officers, dealing with Kosovans seeking asylum in the United Kingdom.

59. He had encountered occasions when he believed relatives passed themselves off for others. These had involved Somali people and White Europeans. This led him to enquire about Mr Husain's relations, as recorded by Ms White.

60. Despite all the litigation about these allegedly false claims in his application, the Tribunal was extremely concerned to see that nothing had been done to 'put the record straight' by the Respondent. Thus, for example, Ms White was unaware until she gave her evidence and was questioned by the Tribunal, that all the substantial points about which doubts had been raised, including the question which she had investigated of whether Mr Husain had successfully applied to pursue a PhD course at the University of Wales, Cardiff, were indisputably accurate. She acknowledged that Mr Husain was entitled to feel highly offended by the contents of her report, if, as it turned out, the contents of his CV and applications were true.

61. At all material times between April 2000 and January 2001, Mr Geoffrey Anderson (A&S Police) and Mr Keith Jackson (A&S Police) were members of a working group to look at the role of Crime Analysts in their Constabulary. As part of their work, they had official contact with Mr Richard Anderson of the Respondent.

Further, Mr Keith Jackson was seconded to the A&S Training Department in March 2000 and undertook a joint Criminal Intelligence Analysis training project with three other officers, including Kent County Constabulary. This required working with Richard Anderson and D/C Russell of the Respondent.

62. In his witness statement and paraphrased in the Reasons of the Bristol Employment Tribunal, Mr Keith Jackson reported that in a discussion during the period from March 2000, Mr Clive Russell mentioned a circulation that he believed Kent County Constabulary had sent to all the UK Police Force Personnel Departments warning them of *"a potentially fraudulent application being made to a number of police for the post of PCIA. This application included USA qualifications that were believed to be fraudulent and the applicant lived somewhere in Wales or the West Country"*. Mr Keith Jackson gave evidence to the Bristol Employment Tribunal. Mr Russell did not. Mr Russell denied that he had made this statement to Mr Jackson. The Tribunal considered that it was more likely than not that Mr Russell had made this comment not least because it served to explain in part A&S's response to Mr Husain's application.

63. The Tribunal also took into account its own view of Mr Husain's application from and the view expressed by D/C White which was that she had not seen anything on the face of the application by Mr Husain which was of concern. She had investigated the issues because she had been asked to do so by her senior officer, Mr Adsley.

64. The successful candidate for the SWP post was a Black woman.

65. In a conversation regarding short listed applicants in October 2000 involving DS Geoffrey Anderson and Keith Jackson (both

of A & S Police), Mr Jackson noted that he had heard of a "bogus" applicant who had applied to the Kent Police. In a conversation around this time, regarding interviewing techniques, DS Geoffrey Anderson of A & S Police mentioned to Richard Anderson, Head Analyst at Kent Police the matter of the "bogus" applicant. He confirmed that it was a reference to the Claimant. DS Geoffrey Anderson subsequently called DC Russell to inquire further.

66. DC White's written report was sent to A & S Special Branch on 4 October 2000.

67. When the Claimant was interviewed by the A & S Police for a job, he was told that if he had not heard of by this date, his application would have been unsuccessful.

68. It appeared that following receipt of the report from Ms White, A & S Police were unable to give the matter their full attention until Sgt Jones of A & S Police instructed DC Colbeck of the same Force to make telephone enquiries regarding DC White's report. Mr Colbeck telephoned Mr Russell of the Kent Police on 5 January 2001 to discuss the contents of DC White's report and also asked him to fax over a copy of the Claimant's application form in 2000. As set out above the arrest followed shortly thereafter.

69. The Respondent's Equal Opportunities Policy which was in force at the time contained a statement that everyone must take responsibility for complying with the principles and rules of the Policy document. It contained a short section dealing with Fair Practice in Recruitment and Selection. This stated that all recruitment of external candidates to the Force would be based on the principle of selecting the most suitable person for the job according to their abilities, experience and qualifications. It required recruitment and selection decisions to be documented

together with the reasons for the decision. It warned against generalized assumptions and stereotyping of candidates and their suitability for a post based on unjustifiable and unsound criteria. In this context it referred to the Force having produced a competency based role requirement for each post. The Policy clearly signalled that a significant means of ensuring that there was no unlawful discrimination in the recruitment process was by applying the Force's selection procedures.

70. Another concern raised was said to be that Mr Husain cited as his employers the Intelligence Bureau in Pakistan at a time when he was living in England. The Tribunal was satisfied that he remained at all material times on extended unpaid leave from his employment. Indeed the Intelligence Bureau wished him to return and to resume his work. In his 1999 application he stated that he wished to settle in the UK and that his children were British citizens, resident here. He had been Deputy Director of the Intelligence Bureau in Karachi, Pakistan since 1998, and had recently been promoted to Director.

71. In the Race Relations Act questionnaire the following question was posed: "12. What is the Respondent's policy for making enquiries in respect of information contained on application forms and/or CVs:

   a. On submission;
   b. After shortlisting; and
   c. On appointment."

72. In the response retuned by the Respondent in November 2004,the following answer was given:

"Kent Police's usual approach to verify the accuracy of information contained within the application form and CV is undertaken by:

i. Discussion at interview through appropriate questioning;
ii. Reference checking; and
iii. Viewing essential documents such as Certificates for Qualifications, Driving Licences, Birth Certificates, etc."

It hardly needs to be recorded that none of these steps was taken in Mr Husain's case.

Submissions

73. In her written opening submission which helpfully set out the Respondent's position on the main legal issues in the case as referred to above, Ms Garner also stated the case in respect of the main allegations against the Respondent. She supplemented these orally at the end of the evidence. As both the written and oral submissions were extensive, the Tribunal will only summarise parts of them in these Reasons. In addition the submissions in respect of the aiding and abetting complaints have been set out earlier in these Reasons. Further Ms Garner compiled a bundle of authorities as follows:

Yearwood—v—Commissioner of Police of the Metropolis [2005] ICR 1660

Igen –v—Wong [2005] IRLR 258

Dresdener Kleinwort Wasserstein Ltd –v Adebayo [2005] IRLR 514

Shamoon –v—Chief Constable of The Royal Ulster Constabulary [2003] IRLR 285

Balamoody-v—UKCNMHV [2002] IRLR 288

Anyanwu –v—South bank Students' Union [2001] IRLR 305

Hallam –v—Avery [2000} ICR 583

Ms Garner also produced for the Tribunal's assistance an extract of the Asylum and Immigration Act 1996. No specific point was made about that Act however.

74. In respect of the first job application, the Respondent did not accept that the Claimant was treated less favourably than other applicants who were white. In relation to the second job application, the Respondent accepted that failing to appoint the Claimant to the position was an act which could result in a finding of race discrimination, in the absence of proof that the decision had nothing to do with the Claimant's race.

75. Ms Garner addressed the question of what evidence there was before the Tribunal to support the Respondent's case that the decisions made in relation to the Claimant were for a reason other than race. She relied on the following in her opening submission:

    75.1 The Respondent operates a recruitment procedure that complied with equal opportunities principles.

    75.2 In respect of the first job application the Claimant was short listed for interview as the qualifications and experience that he set out in his CV and application form demonstrated that he fulfilled the basic requirements for the post.

    75.3 The Claimant was invited to a full interview which included psychometric testing and during which he was judged upon a number of race neutral criteria as set out in the response to the Questionnaire.

75.4 The Claimant was unable to demonstrate at interview the he could fulfil the selection criteria. This was an assessment made by all the interviewers.

75.5 In the subsequent interview in 2000, the Claimant was not shortlisted because of his poor performance at the earlier interview.

75.6 There was concern as there were differences between the qualifications set out on his application form and CV for the two separate applications.

76. At the end of the case this last point was not pursued. The Tribunal has already set out its view about the application on its face. No material difference was put to the Claimant. The Tribunal also bore in mind that it was apparent that the suspicions at the time centred around Mr Husain's US qualifications.

77. In relation to the fifth point, the Tribunal rejected it on the evidence. Not only did Mr Husain's second application to Kent raise new points not contained in his first application, but a fair and unbiased reading of his CV indicated a man who was versatile and able to pick up new skills in the course of his career. The Respondent would not have known this at the material times, but Mr Husain's subsequent training and employment history in this country has borne this out also.

Conclusions

78. In assessing the complaint in respect of the 1999 application, the Tribunal considered whether the primary facts shifted the burden of proof on to the shoulders of the Respondent. It was not in dispute that the Claimant had submitted an excellent paper

application which secured him an interview; he had relevant experience; and he is of Pakistani racial origin. The Tribunal, in the absence of detail relating to the Claimant's interview and that of the successful candidate, for reasons set out above, had to determine whether the Claimant had established primary facts such that the burden shifted to the Respondent to satisfy the Tribunal that the Claimant's failure to be appointed in 1999 was not on racial grounds.

79. The Tribunal considered that the Respondent should have made a far more extensive search for relevant documents in 2001 when proceedings were issued. In a complaint such as this the file of the successful candidate was always going to be material.

80. The Tribunal accepted Mr Husain's contention that he was told at the time that he came a 'close second'. However the Tribunal also found that his subsequent application in 2000 was more relevant; and by then Mr Husain had been able to read up more about the job. The Tribunal took into account the record of the assessment of Mr Husain complied at the time. It was also relevant that at the time Mr Husain perceived nothing amiss, and indeed renewed his application to work for Kent in 2000. He made no criticism of the process either at the time or subsequently.

81. Taking all these matters into account the Tribunal could not find that the Claimant had been the best candidate in fact and thus could not conclude that the burden of disproving race had shifted to the Respondent in respect of the 1999 selection.

82. In April 2000 Mr Anderson withdrew the Claimant from the selection process. The burden of disproving race discrimination in respect of the 2000 application moved to the Respondent.

83. The explanation provided by the Respondent that this was related to the Claimant's poor performance in 1999 at interview was rejected by the Tribunal. Mr R Anderson's attempt to cloak his action of withdrawing Mr Husain's application from the process as being in line with the Respondent's prevailing personnel practices at the time was also significant. The tribunal also took into account Mr R Anderson's unjustified response to the Claimant's 2000 application of setting in train an investigation by Mr Russell rather than letting the application run its course and checking the qualifications in accordance with the Respondent's stated usual practice. Further, the contemplation of criminal proceedings in relation to this matter was also highly material in the Tribunal's view.

84. This appeared to the Tribunal to be a gross overreaction to any concerns or suspicions about the contents of the Claimant's application. If there were questions about the accuracy of the information in the application, it would have been more straightforward for the Claimant to be progressed to the next stage in 2000 and for him and all other short listed candidates to be asked to produce confirmatory evidence of their qualifications and experience. If the information on the application had been viewed fairly, even if Mr Husain had not been successful on the previous occasion, the Tribunal considered that the expected course would have been that he would have been interviewed again if he passed the sift criteria, and he could have demonstrated at interview whether or not he could do the job, relative to those being considered at that stage. The withdrawal of the Claimant's application from the normal recruitment process, contrary to the procedure which was meant to ensure equal opportunity, for no good reason, raised the question whether the action was taken on racial grounds.

85. Given Mr Anderson's background of developing new policies on recruitment, the Tribunal considered that it was more surprising that

he did not comply with the procedures. The Tribunal considered that Mr Anderson knowingly stepped outside of the Respondent's procedures at the time. That decision by him was not satisfactorily explained by him.

86. The Tribunal rejected the explanation that Mr Husain's performance in 1999 was poor. Even if it had been, the Tribunal did not consider that this was a good reason for failing to give him a second chance, when such a withdrawal from the process was not the normal procedure. In any event, there may have been many explanations for a poor performance at interview in 1999, even if that had been the case.

87. The Tribunal also rejected Mr Anderson's evidence that the second application showed no development as compared to the first. This was patently incorrect, as the Tribunal has found.

88. Far from being reassured by the Respondent's evidence that race was not a determining factor in 2000, the Tribunal concluded that the Respondent had not discharged the burden of proving that they had not discriminated against the Claimant on racial grounds.

89. The next point considered was the complaint that the applications to South Wales Police and to the Avon & Somerset Police were acts of discrimination. The Tribunal considered these complaints along with the aiding and abetting complaints. The Tribunal accepted the contentions of the Respondent that as a matter of law the Tribunal could not find that they had aided and abetted the two other Police Forces in respect of matters that had not been found to be acts of race discrimination. This in the Tribunal's view meant that the complaint of siding and abetting the Avon and Somerset Police could not succeed, having been the subject of a Tribunal judgment following a hearing of the merits. The primary question

of the liability of the A & S Police could also not be a matter for this Tribunal, having been dealt with by the Bristol Tribunal. Both the complaints of race discrimination by A & S Police and of the Respondent aiding and abetting the A & S Police were therefore not well founded and were dismissed.

90. The position of the South Wales Police was somewhat different. That claim had been dismissed because the Cardiff Tribunal lacked jurisdiction to determine it, having regard to the time which had elapsed since the rejection of the Claimant's application. Despite that however this Tribunal considered itself unable to conclude, on the limited evidence before it, that there had been a primary act of race discrimination by the South Wales Police. The documents and evidence before the Tribunal made it clear that DC White of South Wales Police in or about May 2000 when Mr Husain applied for the job, like the A&S Police later, relied very heavily on what she was told by Mr Russell of the Kent Police about Mr Husain. However the Tribunal heard no evidence from Mr Adsley, the person in South Wales Police who initiated the enquiry by DC White into Mr Husain's application, therefore the had no way of determining whether the decision to set those enquiries in train was racially discriminatory, or was in any way influence by the Kent Police's view of Mr Husain at this time.

91. In all those circumstances therefore the complaints of direct race discrimination by the South Wales Police and of the Respondent aiding and abetting that Force were not well founded and were dismissed.

92. The next complaint was made under paragraph 10(b) of the Particulars of Discrimination dated 31 march 2004. Given the Tribunal's earlier findings and conclusions in this case, and in particular Mr Russell's communication to other Forces and

73

criminal charges were being contemplated by the Respondent, and Mr R Anderson's discussions with officers from other Forces, the Tribunal considered that the Claimant had established that he had been depicted as a criminal and d deceit by the Respondent. The tribunal was not satisfied that the Respondent had discharged the burden of proving that this had not been done on racial grounds. The Tribunal has already referred to its views about the comments surrounding the Northumbria Police course in this context. The utter baselessness of the points relating to the Claimant's qualifications is also relevant, as is the fact that the Respondent did no check these points by the normal means of asking the candidate for verification. This complaint therefore succeeded.

93. In paragraph 10© of the Particulars of Discrimination, Mr Husain complained that the "utter falsity and baseless of each of the allegations of criminal deception" made against him were acts of discrimination. The Tribunal agreed that there was no basis whatsoever for the allegations of criminal deception. However, the Tribunal considered that this paragraph was in truth a statement of points which the Claimant believed were relevant to other allegations of race discrimination, as opposed to a substantive act of discrimination. It was not an allegation of an act or omission. No finding of liability was made in respect of this paragraph, but the points made informed the Tribunal's findings on the other paragraphs.

94. In paragraph 10(d), Mr Husain complained about the "totally perfunctory nature of the investigations" conducted by all the officers of varying ranks over a period of one and half years, all of whom were White. The Tribunal considered it could only reach findings about the actions of the Respondent's officers or staff, for the reasons set out above in relations to the claims of discrimination against the other Forces.

95. The Tribunal agreed that the investigations by Mr Russell were totally perfunctory, and considered that the facts established by the Claimant of such erroneous results, mocking comments about the participation on the Police course and the difference of race shifted the burden onto the Respondent. The Respondent had done nothing to put the record straight once it became clear from the A & S investigation that the Claimant's application contained truthful representations. Mr Russell was said to be a very experienced detective constable, formerly of the Special branch. The Respondent did not argue that he was generally incompetent.

96. The Tribunal considered that once charged with the investigation, Mr Russell adopted stereotypical adverse assumptions about Mr Husain as a Pakistani which led him to conduct his enquiries of the Massachusetts Institute of Technology and with the Northumbria Police in a very casual manner. The Tribunal considers that the mocking terms in which the participation on the course was erroneously reported further attests to this. Even at the Tribunal hearing when Mr Russell was aware that Mr Husain was contending that he was mistaken, there was a complete absence of sympathy or regret on Mr Russell's part of the consequences of his actions.

97. On the basis of the evidence presented and the facts found, the Tribunal concluded that the respondent had failed to adduce cogent evidence which discharged the burden of proving that the perfunctory investigation was not on racial grounds.

98. The complaints in paragraphs 10 (e) and (f) of the Particulars of Discrimination related to the actions of and conduct by the A & S Police in arresting and interrogating the Claimant. As the substantive complaints of race discrimination had already been dealt with by the Bristol Employment Tribunal, they were not

matters that the Tribunal could adjudicate upon. These complaints were therefore dismissed.

99. Finally, Mr Husain complained of collusion between the Police Forces resulting in the contamination of his applications for employment. The notoriety given to Mr Husain's application by Mr Russell and Mr Anderson was based on the assessment that he was not a genuine contender for the posts he applied for based on fabricated qualifications and experience. The Tribunal considered that there was not a proper basis for reaching that conclusion about Mr Husain, even if, which the Tribunal did not accept, his 1999 interview had been poor.

100. This complaint was well founded in so far as it complained of the numerous occasions on which Mr Russell and Mr R Anderson passed on their suspicions about Mr Husain and the results of Mr Russell's enquiries, which the Tribunal had found to be acts of race discrimination. It was clear that this information affected the A & S Police application. It was less clear on the available evidence, as set out above, whether this information influenced the South Wales Police application.

Chairman
Ms C Hyde

31 October 2005
RESERVED JUDGMENT
JUDGMENT SENT TO THE
PARTIES ON
31 October 2005
AND ENTERED IN THE REGISTER
FOR SECRETARY OF THE
TRIBUNALS

RESERVED JUDGMENT

THE EMPLOYMENT TRIBUNAL

SITTING AT: ASHFORD, KENT
BEFORE: Ms C Hyde
MEMBERS: Mr M J Blackwell
                           Mr T J Gallagher

BETWEEN:

Mr Shujaat Husain   Claimant

And

The Chief Constable of   Respondent
Kent County Constabulary

ON: 15 December 2005 and
                 (in chambers on 8 February 2006)

Appearances:

For the Claimant: In person, assisted by Miss L Connerty
                        Acting as a McKenzie's friend

For the Respondent: Miss S Garner, Counsel

REMEDY JUDGMENT

The unanimous Judgment of the Tribunal is that:

1. As the Respondent's application for a review was not pursued, no order was made in respect of it.

2. The Tribunal excluded from its consideration a letter sent from the Respondent's legal department to Counsel in the current litigation.

3. The Tribunal made the following recommendations:

    3.1 The Chief Constable of Kent Police provides Mr Husain with a written apology in terms consistent with the findings of this Tribunal within 28 days of the date of this judgment.

    3.2 That the Respondent formulates an action plan within six months of the date of this judgment, after seeking advice from the Commission for Racial Equality, with the aim of preventing any repetition of the shortcomings relating to the recruitment process which occurred in the case.

4. The Respondent was ordered to pay to Claimant the sum of **£65,746.73** in total in respect of compensation for racial discrimination (injury to feelings, aggravated and exemplary damages, past loss of earning and future loss of earnings); and interest thereon.

5. No award was made in respect of personal injury.

REASONS

1. Reasons are provided for this judgment in respect of remedy as those matters were reserved. Judgment was given orally in respect of the review and the disclosure issue at the hearing on 15 December 2005.

2. The Tribunal heard evidence from Mr Husain [witness statement C3] on his own behalf. On behalf of the Respondent Mr Richard

Anderson and Ms Diana Harris gave evidence [witness statement in R1].

3.   The Respondent had prepared a bundle of documents for the remedy hearing [R1] as had the Claimant [C1]. The Respondent also produced a further document [R2] which calculated future loss on alternative bases to ages 60 and 65.

4.   The Tribunal decided not to consider the further representations sent in by the Claimant's McKenzie's Friend after the hearing on 15 December 2005. This further evidence had not been sent in with the leave of the Tribunal, it was sent in just prior to the chambers hearing on 8 February 2006 and no comments on this course had apparently been obtained from the Respondent. At the hearing the Tribunal excluded from its considerations a letter sent by the Respondent to the Claimant in error. The letter was clearly the subject of professional privilege. The Tribunal did not consider that the circumstance in which it had been disclosed indicated an intention to waive privilege, nor was its disclosure necessary for the fair determination of the issues in the case.

The Issues

5.   Both parties had prepared separate written submissions in respect of the Respondent's application for a review which was in the end not pursued, given clarification from the Tribunal as to the effect of the liability judgment and reasons and written submission in respect of the substantive remedy issues. The Respondent's submission on the substantive remedy issues was some eight pages long and the Respondent also produced copies of relevant cases as follows: **HM Prison Service v Salmon [2001] IRLR 425; Essa v Laing Ltd [2004] IRLR 313; Vento v Chief Constable of West Yorkshire Police (2) [2003] IRLR 102.**

6. The main issues that the Tribunal had to consider were:

   6.1 Awards for the injury to feelings, aggravated and exemplary damages, personal injury.

   6.2 Past loss of earnings award

   6.3 Future loss of earnings award

   6.4 Award of interest

   6.5 Recommendations.

7. The issue in respect of injury to feelings apart from deciding what was the appropriate award was also whether the discrimination found had caused the injury to feelings claimed. The Claimant relied on medical evidence which the Respondent submitted related to loss which was not caused by the discrimination found. The Respondent distinguished between the issue of what injury was foreseeable and that which was caused by the discrimination.

Submissions

8. As the submissions were committed to writing the Tribunal only sets them out in these Reasons in summary form. The Respondent submitted that the Tribunal should be careful to apportion any award for injury to feelings separately from any award for personal injury. Miss Garner relied on the judgment in **HM Prison Service v Salmon** (above) which indicated that such a breakdown should generally be made.

9. In respect of the injury to feelings claim she referred the Tribunal to the **Vento** and **Salmon** cases and distinguished the nature of the discrimination found in those cases from the discrimination in the current case.

10. Miss Garner then addressed the issue of causation. She acknowledged that it was abundantly apparent that Mr Husain felt extremely aggrieved as a result of the treatment he received. She did not seek to challenge on behalf of the Respondent that his feelings were genuine. However, she urged the Tribunal to consider that in making an award for injury to feelings in accordance with the case of **Salmon,** to consider the extent to which the Claimant's feelings were due to the acts of the Respondent and the extent to which they were attributable to other matters, i.e.

   (a) Acts of other parties e.g. the other two police forces involved;

   (b) Matters that were ruled out of time (e.g. the Cardiff claim);

   (c) Matters considered but rejected by the Tribunal in the current claim. In particular she drew the Tribunal's attention to all the allegations in the particulars of aiding and abetting which had not been made out.

11. She referred the Tribunal to the judgment in the case of **Essa v Laing** which dealt with whether the foreseeability of the extent of injury should be considered by a Tribunal. She submitted that it was noted that a Respondent did not have to foresee the extent of the injury for it to be recoverable. However, to guard against damages that may appear to be too remote it was said in response to submissions that a control mechanism beyond that of causation was needed, "reliance on the good sense of Employment Tribunals in finding the facts and reaching conclusions on them is . . . sufficient . . .": paragraph 37 of the Judgment.

12. Miss Garner then drew the Tribunal's attention to various factors in the Liability Judgment and which arose from the circumstances

of the case which she submitted placed considerable bounds on the extent to which the Respondent should be liable for all the injuries the Claimant had suffered.

13. Miss Garner also addressed the period of time which had elapse before the claim to the hearing. His was not a matter which could be attributed to the actions of the Respondent. The delay was due to the hearings against the other two Respondent and the decision to appeal the Cardiff decision to the EAT twice and to the Court of Appeal once. Miss Garner suggested that the 'blame' for the Claimant's injured feelings should be split between the three Forces involved so far as causation od damage was concerned as follows: South Wales – 15%, the Respondent – 15% and Avon and Somerset – 70%.

14. She invited the Tribunal to consider the loss attributable to the Respondent by looking at the effect of intervening acts on its actions. She submitted that the actions of South Wales and Avon and Somerset Police were intervening acts which exacerbated the Claimant's injury to feelings to an extent way over and above that which would have been experienced had the matter simply remained as a failed job interview and a series of perfunctory investigations. She reminded the Tribunal that it had been decided in the case of **Ministry of Defence v Cannock [1994] IRLR 509** that it was wrong for awards for injury to feelings to be used as a means of deterring employers from particular courses of conduct.

15. In respect of the personal injury claim the Respondent submitted that the medical reports did not provide evidence as to the causation of Mr Husain's conditions and therefore it was submitted that this claim should fail.

16. Miss Garner next addressed the issue of aggravated damages. She referred the Tribunal to the circumstances in which such an award may be made. She submitted that DC Russell's behaviour fell short of that which was required for an award of aggravated damages. She further submitted that the conduct of the Respondent in dealing with the litigation had not been "wholly inappropriate and intimidatory". She referred to the evidence that was placed before the Tribunal as to the difficulty that the Respondent experienced regarding the documentation and the evidence of Mr Kirk at the liability hearing and the Judgment of Mr Zuke on this issue on 3 December 2001. She acknowledged that the Respondent had not acted as promptly as it should have done e.g. in the provision of a response to the questionnaire. However, she submitted that this matter had been taken into account when the Tribunal considered liability.

17. Finally she referred the Tribunal to examples of cases where aggravated damages were awarded and to the level of such awards e.g. in the cases of **Vento** and **Salmon.**

18. It was not in dispute that the Tribunal was entitled to make an award of exemplary damages. Miss Garner referred to the Judgment in the case of **Kuddus v Chief Constable of Leicestershire Constabulary [2001] WLR 1789.** The Tribunal had to be satisfied that compensation was insufficient to punish the Respondent and that the conduct of the Respondent constituted oppressive, arbitrary or unconstitutional action by the agents of Government. Miss Garner submitted that compensation was likely to be adequate in this case and also that the conduct of DC Russell fell short of 'oppressive' or 'arbitrary' and was not unconstitutional. The fact that it was discriminatory conduct did not of itself amount to unconstitutional conduct. There had to be something more, it was suggested.

19. In respect of the loss of earnings Miss Garner submitted that the Claimant would have to show that he would have been given the job. The Respondent submitted that:

    a. The Claimant would not have succeeded at interview; and
    b. The Claimant has not proved that he would have succeeded at the vetting stage.

20. Miss Garner then drew the Tribunal's attention to various matters which she submitted supported these contentions.

21. In respect of the claim for past loss of earnings the Claimant contended that he had only been able to earn £30,000 over the past five years and eight months since the act of discrimination. He contended that this would increase to just £10,000 per annum for the rest of his working life. The Respondent contended that this was not an accurate reflection of what Mr Husain should be earning because:

    a. He had applied for and maintained that he should have been appointed to a position with a gross salary of over £18,000 per annum; and
    b. The Tribunal expressed the view in its Judgment that he was a 'man who was versatile and able to pick up new skills in the course of his career".

22. She contended that Mr Husain had provided no evidence to show applications for full time positions outside the fields of policing or intelligence despite his arguments that his career within policing in the United Kingdom was doomed. This led Miss Garner to submit that the Claimant had provided insufficient evidence or mitigation of loss and that any award should be reduced to reflect the fact

that 12 months after the act complained of Mr Husain should have obtained alternative employment at a rate of pay comparable to that of the post applied for.

23. The Claimant had provided no evidence to show that he was medically incapable of doing so.

24. Miss Garner made a further submission in relation to interest.

25. To his submissions, Mr Husain appended the judgments in the cases of **Chief Constable of West Yorkshire Police v Khan (House of Lords)** and **Kuddus v Chief Constable of Leicestershire Constabulary,** and **Zaiwalla and another v Walia (Employment Appeal Tribunal).**

26. Mr Husain commenced his submission by summarising the discrimination suffered by him. He referred to the Tribunal's specific finding that he had been racially discriminated against in respect of :

   26.1 The rejection of his job application in April 2000.
   26.2 The depiction of him as a criminal who should be arrested and criminally prosecuted.
   26.3 The perfunctory investigations made into his background by the Respondent.
   26.4 The contamination of his application for employment with Avon and Somerset Police Force due to collusion between the Respondent and that Force.

27. In respect of loss of earnings Mr Husain submitted that he would have succeeded in his job application but for the discriminatory acts of the Respondent and he did not accept that only a chance of employment was lost. He thus claimed loss of earnings for the

post of Intelligence Officer at the salary stated in his schedule of loss. He believed he was entitled to annual increments. Further, he submitted that but for the discriminatory actions of the Respondent he would have succeeded in obtaining an equivalent post with a UK Police Force in or around May/June 2000 and claimed such loss of earnings accordingly.

28. In respect of future earnings Mr Husain submitted that he would have succeeded in his April 2000 application for employment or in an equivalent application for employment made shortly thereafter and would have proceeded through the ranks and remained in employment with the Police until retirement. He was now 50 years old and due to the actions of the Respondent had no future with any UK Police Force. His future employment would consist of such teaching and examining jobs as he had been able to obtain in the past four and a half years and his claim for future loss of earnings was calculated accordingly.

29. Mr Husain stated that he had a deep respect for the UK Police and a strong desire to obtain employment with them. However, he believed the Respondent had destroyed his chances of obtaining such employment and caused him to suffer humiliation, embarrassment, loss of dignity, reputation and self-esteem. He contended that he had been traumatised by the Respondent's actions and his family life had suffered in consequence. He believed that this was a truly exceptional case justifying an award considerably in excess of the bands set out in the **Vento** case.

30. In respect of his personal injury claim he submitted that he had suffered from angina and diabetes and that the discriminatory action of the Respondent and the stress of the long running and contentious litigation had caused him trauma and that such trauma

had considerably worsened these conditions and affected his health and his family life.

31. Mr Husain then turned to address the issue of aggravated damages. He referred to the relevant authority of **Zaiwalla** above. He submitted that the test had been met in this case, justifying an award **of aggr**avated damages by reference to the Respondent's actions in respect of the perfunctory investigation into his background and the depiction of him as a criminal who should be arrested and criminally prosecuted.

32. He submitted that the discriminatory acts were akin to libel, negligence and misfeasance in a public office and that his damages should reflect this.

33. He also referred to the fact that the litigation had been protracted and contentious and to the stress that he had suffered as a result. He submitted that in this case the actions of the Respondent and their representatives went beyond the permitted "robust" defence: **Khan** above.

34. The Claimant addressed the Tribunal on the appropriateness of an award for exemplary damages. He submitted that the Respondent was a highly trained and resourced institution providing a public service. As such higher standards of integrity must be demanded of them in the carrying out of their work. He submitted that all discriminatory acts that the Respondent committed fell far short of the standards, but in particular their depiction of the Claimant as a criminal and insultingly perfunctory investigation into his background illustrated the positive misuse of their training and power of investigation and deduction. Their conduct had been truly "arbitrary and outrageous use of executive power" based on racial grounds.

35. He further submitted that exemplary damages were justified in this case in the hope that their punitive effect may act as an eye-opener to the Respondent and their representatives in respect of what he contended was an indication of the Respondent's disrespectful attitude towards the Tribunal illustrated by Mr Richard Anderson's statement prepared for the remedy hearing. He made references to various sections of Mr Anderson's witness statement and the contempt of the Tribunal's findings. He specifically referred to various parts of the Tribunal's judgment.

36. Mr Husain also sought recommendations. These were that:

   a. The Chief Constable of Kent Police provides him with a written apology in terms to be agreed and does this together with the issue of a press release in terms to be agreed and does so at a press conference arranged for the purpose.
   b. That the Respondent investigates the conduct of the individual Officers concerned with a view to bringing disciplinary sanctions for further deterrence.
   c. That the Police Complaints Authority investigates the actions of the Respondent which have been found to be discriminatory.
   d. That the Law Society and the Bar Council investigate the actions and conduct of the Respondent's legal representatives in their conduct of the litigation, particularly with regard to abuse of public funds, wrong or poor advice and in needless aggravation of the matter over several years.

37. In discussing the issues with the parties the Tribunal clarified that as far as interest was concerned the appropriate rate applied in full to the injury to feelings award and general damages but applied at half the rate in respect of any award for specific financial loss.

Conclusions and Additional Findings of Fact

38. The Tribunal considered each of the heads of remedy in turn. The Tribunal has already set out its findings on liability in respect of which remedy was being determined.

39. The first free-standing matter that the Tribunal considered was the Claimant's claim for personal injuries. The Tribunal agreed with the Respondent that it is necessary for a Claimant to prove that the injury claimed has been caused by the discrimination found to have occurred. On the basis of the evidence presented by the Claimant, including the medical evidence at pages 66 to 68 of his bundle, there was an insufficient evidential basis to establish the causation of the Claimant's hypertension or diabetes mellitus. The evidence before the Tribunal was in any event unclear in terms of the chronology of the onset of each condition.

40. The Tribunal next considered the question of compensation for injury to feelings. The judgments in the cases of **Armitage** and **Vento** were reviewed. The Tribunal was careful to consider what injury to feelings was caused by the actions of this Respondent (and not any other person). The circumstances of this case were unusual. The experience of the rejection of his job application in April 2000 did not of itself elicit a perception in the Claimant at the time that he had been discriminated against. It was the subsequent discovery of the circumstances surrounding that rejection and the other matters in January 2001 that led to his feelings being injured. The Tribunal considered that it was appropriate to assess the period of injured feelings from the date of his interview with Avon and Somerset Police for this reason.

41. The Tribunal also considered separately the period which had elapsed between the acts of discrimination between April 2000 up to about the first part of 2001, and the subsequent four year delay before the Tribunal gave its judgment in respect of liability. The Tribunal accepted the submission of Miss Garner that a large part of these delays were not attributable to the Respondent. The Tribunal decided to award interest for such period s it would normally take for a claim of this complexity to come to a remedy hearing. In the Tribunal's experience this would not normally exceed two years. The Tribunal accepted that the Respondent did not actively protract the proceedings. An award of interest for a longer period would penalise the Respondent. Interest on general damages therefore ran for two years from January 2001.

42. The Tribunal gave very careful consideration to the submissions relating to causation. The Tribunal was firmly of the view that the actions of Avon and Somerset were separate actions in themselves albeit that they were occasioned by information gleaned from Kent. The Tribunal took into account its findings that Avon and Somerset had reverted to Kent and had checked with Kent about their information before proceeding with the action that they took. They also fully informed Kent of the reason why they were checking with them. The Tribunal considered that without the information from Kent in the first place and then subsequently emphasised or reinforced by Kent, it was doubtful that Avon and Somerset would have proceeded to arrest the Claimant. The Tribunal did not consider that this was inconsistent with the finding of the Bristol Employment Tribunal that Avon and Somerset were acting in good faith on the information received. The Tribunal considered that the Respondent's actions and omissions substantially contributed to the arrest and questioning by Avon and Somerset Police in January 2001.

90

43. The Tribunal considered that as Kent was aware of the reason for the Avon and Somerset's enquiries and the actions of Avon and Somerset proposed to take, they must bear some responsibility for the consequences of their actions or omissions albeit that Kent did not actively pursue the arrest. This was the context in which the Tribunal had reached its findings that the Respondent had colluded with Avon and Somerset. It had provided information and assistance to Avon and Somerset in full knowledge of the reasons why Avon and Somerset sought the information but, reckless or negligent as to the consequences of its actions, if not actually deliberate.

44. The Tribunal thus disagreed with the submission at paragraph 1.95 of the Respondent's document in which Miss Garner submitted that there was no evidence whatsoever that the Respondent had any knowledge of what Avon and Somerset Force was planning to do. The Tribunal referred to paragraphs 56, 61, 62, 65 and 68 of its Reasons in the Liability Judgment.

45. On the other hand, given the circumstances of the way in which this case evolved and the evidence before the Tribunal, the Tribunal had relatively little information about the role of the South Wales Police and the information obtained by DC White without regard to Kent. The Tribunal also reminded itself that the actions of South Wales Police were not discriminatory in accordance with the findings of the Cardiff Tribunal.

46. The Tribunal reminded itself that the conclusion of DC White's report in May 2000 was that South Wales Police should not employ the Claimant. There was no view expressed as to the bringing of a criminal prosecution.

47. Similarly, the Tribunal reminded itself that the actions of the Avon and Somerset Police which unquestionably had a severe impact on Mr Husain had also been found not to be discriminatory.

48. In assessing the award for injury to feelings, the Tribunal considered each of the findings that it had made. The effect of the discrimination in respect of the April 2000 job rejection was that Mr Richard Anderson took the Claimant completely out of the running for a job, without good reason. The Tribunal had in mind the figure £5,000 for the injured feelings suffered by Mr Husain by reason of having been removed from consideration for a position which he had come close to being appointed previously. The difficulty in awarding a separate figure in respect of the job application is that the Claimant found out about this discrimination at the same time as he perceived the matters found at paragraphs 26.2-4 above. It was therefore artificial to seek to make separate awards in respect of each act of discrimination.

49. Turning to the question of the Claimant's chances of getting the job in April 2000, taking all matters into account the Tribunal considered that his chances of getting this job in April 2000 stood at 25%. The Tribunal took into account the evidence which the Respondent gave at the remedy hearing of other candidates whose immigration status had needed to be regularised or altered. This had not been a bar to their being employed by the Respondent.

50. It was once again highly regrettable that the Tribunal had no reliable information reliable about the successful candidate or about the pool of candidates that the Claimant was competing in. The Tribunal also had no information as to the number of candidates.

51. The Tribunal considered that the previous competition in 1999 was of some, but limited value. There were no proper grounds for concluding that the pool was the same or similar to that in April 2000. The Tribunal however took into account its findings that the Claimant would have been short-listed, i.e. he would have met the criteria for short-listing in 2000 also, and that in 1999 Mr Husain came a close second. Against that the Tribunal had evidence that the Claimant had not secured another Intelligence Analyst post in another Force at about the time concerned in circumstances which the Tribunal had to treat as non-discriminatory. The Claimant was for example short-listed for posts in Grampian Police and Teesside.

52. Further, it was relevant that the Claimant as the Tribunal found had taken steps to improve his application to Kent in 2000. Having regard to all those circumstances and to the somewhat delayed injury to feelings, the Tribunal considered that Mr Husain, once he found out, was extremely distressed by the fact that by reason of his race he had not been given an opportunity to compete for the Analyst's job in Kent.

53. When assessing the lost earnings claim, the Tribunal had to consider the Respondent's argument that the Claimant's chances of getting the job were severely reduced because of his immigration status. During the liability hearing, the Tribunal was taken to a letter at page 106 of the liability bundle indicating that as of 15 October 2000 the Claimant was being called to a meeting to be given a National Insurance number due to his commencing employment.

54. Mr Husain was born in November 1955. The Tribunal had to assess what was the likelihood of his remaining employed with

the Respondent if he had obtained the position. The Tribunal considered that there were two very powerful arguments as to why the Claimant would have remained in that employment. He would have been doing what he enjoyed and what was consistent with his professional life up to that date and, second, his age was working against him in terms of securing other work of a similar status and appropriateness. The Tribunal found it impossible, however, to say that the Claimant would have advanced beyond the position applied for of Intelligence Analyst. There was no proper evidence or basis for determining this issue.

55. In considering the loss of earnings therefore, the Tribunal considered that there was an actual loss from the beginning of September 2000 to the calculation date in February 2006, a period of five years, five months.

£18,711.78 gross = £13,949.88 net per annum

Loss of earnings for five years and five
Months at that rate = £75,561.85

25% of that = **£11,390.46**

Interest on £11,390.46 at 3% for five years, five months = **£1850.90**

Future Loss

56. The Claimant claimed future loss to retirement at the age of 65. The Tribunal had regard to the further document [R2] produced by the Respondent which calculated future loss on alternative bases to ages 60 and 65. This document also set out the relevant multiplier under the Ogden tables.

57. The Claimant was not cross-examined on his contention that he would have remained to retirement at 65. The Tribunal has already set out its conclusion to the likelihood of the Claimant remaining in secure employment once he found it.

58. The Tribunal therefore took a as the relevant multiplier 12.74 (in respect of retirement age of 65). This gave a figure of £17,771.47.

   From this the Tribunal deducted the sum of £10,000 per annum with a multiplier of 12.74 = £127,400

   The Tribunal further reduced the award to reflect its findings that the Claimant had a 25% chance of securing the employment = **£12,580.37** = future loss.

59. No interest was to be awarded on the award for future loss of earnings.

60. The Tribunal then reverted to the question of injury to feelings at points 2, 3, and 4 of the judgment, taking into account the Claimant's hurt feelings at the discrimination. The Tribunal considered that Respondent had a pivotal role in causing the Claimant's arrest, thus rendering the Respondent liable to compensate the Claimant for the loss suffered.

Injury to feelings

61. Given the Claimant's professional background and age and personality, and his accounts of the effect of the discrimination on him, the Tribunal had little hesitation in estimating that the injury to feelings award fell in the high bracket. The Tribunal awarded

the sum of **£25,000** in respect of injured feelings for the total discrimination suffered.

62. The Tribunal assessed interest on the injured feelings for the period of two years from 10 January 2001 at 6% (the agreed rate) per annum x 2 years = **£3,000.**

Aggravated Damages

63. The Tribunal next considered the claim for aggravated damages. DC Colbeck, the officer in the Avon and Somerset Police who investigated Mr Husain's application form prepared a reported dated 25 January 2001 in which he set out the outcome of his enquiries and the conclusion that there were no grounds for believing that Mr Husain had misrepresented his qualifications and background. The Tribunal was strongly of the view that Mr Colbeck's report should have led the Respondent at least to apologise to Mr Husain for its role in bringing about the sequence of events which led to his arrest. It was not until the beginning of the remedy hearing that the Respondent through their Counsel, for the first time indicated tot eh Tribunal that a letter of apology had been drafted and was awaiting the Chief Constable's return from leave for signature. This apology was prepared after receipt of the liability judgment. The Tribunal considered that the Respondent should have been much more alive at a much earlier stage to the likely distress caused to Mr Husain. An apology could have been provided without any suggestion of liability for race discrimination. The Respondent was also in full possession of the details of Mr Husain's background, which should have indicated to the Respondent that he would have found it particularly difficult to have been arrested for or even suspected of fraudulent representation.

64. The Tribunal reminded itself of its earlier finding that it was not the Respondent's fault that the litigation had been protracted. The delay, however, did not assist the Respondent in this regard because it should have provided even more opportunity for the Respondent to assess this aspect. The Tribunal considered that the absence of an apology from Kent over a four year period aggravated the injured feelings as perceived by Mr Husain. The Tribunal awarded a further sum of **£4,000.**

Exemplary Damages

65. The Tribunal next considered the claim for exemplary damages. Mr Husain presented himself to Kent as a potential civilian employee. Their discrimination exposed him to the risk of criminal prosecution. Mr Husain was put in that position because of the way the prospective employer chose to exercise its wider powers. The Tribunal contrasted the actions of Kent with the actions of South Wales Police as reflected by the careful recommendation in Ms White's report that South Wales Police did not employ the Claimant. Given that the Respondent use its police background to conduct what the Tribunal found to be a perfunctory investigation, the Tribunal considered that this was a case in which the conditions for the making of an exemplary award were satisfied.

66. Further it was important that the Claimant was adequately compensated. These matters were separate from the considerations which gave rise to an award for aggravated damages. The Tribunal did not consider that the award of £25,000 to the Claimant was adequate and increased the award by a further **£5,000** for exemplary damages.

67. The Tribunal awarded interest on the awards of exemplary damages (£5,000) and aggravated damages (£4,000) at the rate of 6% per annum for the period of five years and five months = **£2,925.**

68. The grand total of the award therefore is in the sum of **£65,746.73.**

Chairman

Ms C Hyde

28 March 2006

RESERVED JUDGMENT

JUDGEMENT SENT TO THE PARTIES ON

30 March 2006

AND ENTERED IN THE REGISTER

About the Author

Shujaat Husain is an ex-career police officer from the Pakistan police. He is a double honours graduate from the well-known Massachusetts Institute of Technology in the United States, which he attended in the late 1970s on scholarship. After working for a few years in the private sector, he joined the Pakistan Police Service. He left in 1999 and moved to Britain in 1999 for family reasons.

In efforts to resume his career with the police, he applied for jobs that suited his background. The saga that ensued has been documented quite vividly in his memoirs. That work, *Are British Police Institutionally Racist? Memoirs of an Accused Conman* should be an eye-opener for those who deny the shortcomings of the British police and also for future job aspirants who hail from minorities.

A rated chess and bridge player, Husain now teaches and examines A-Level subjects. He lives in South London. Occasionally, he also writes political commentary on current topics.